I0488490

Copyright © 2015 Sarah Robert & Randolph Rubicon

All Rights Reserved Worldwide

CREATURES OF THE NIGHT

&

POPULAR TALES

COLORING BOOK
2 BOOK BUNDLE

CREATURES
Of The Night

Horror Coloring Book

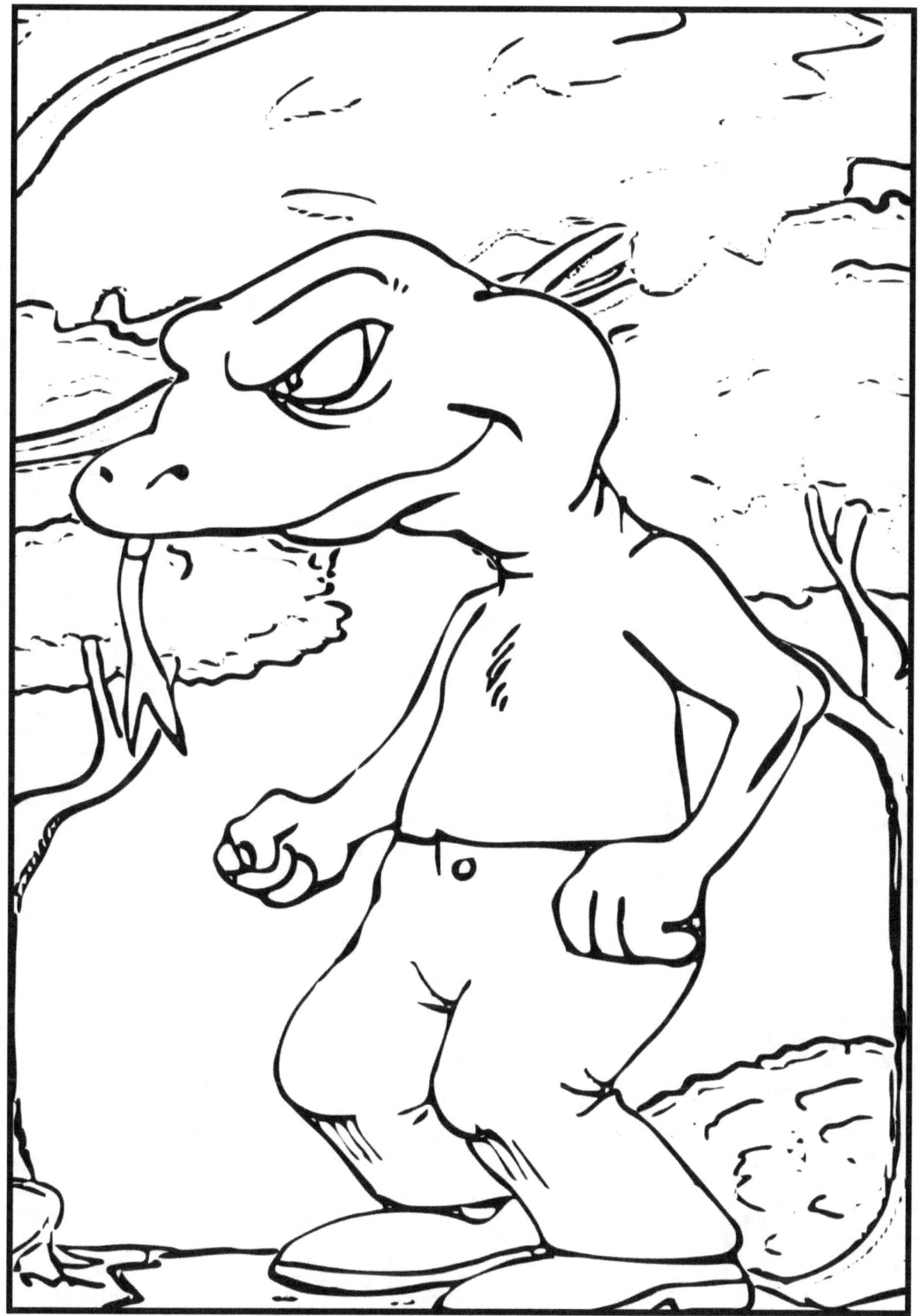

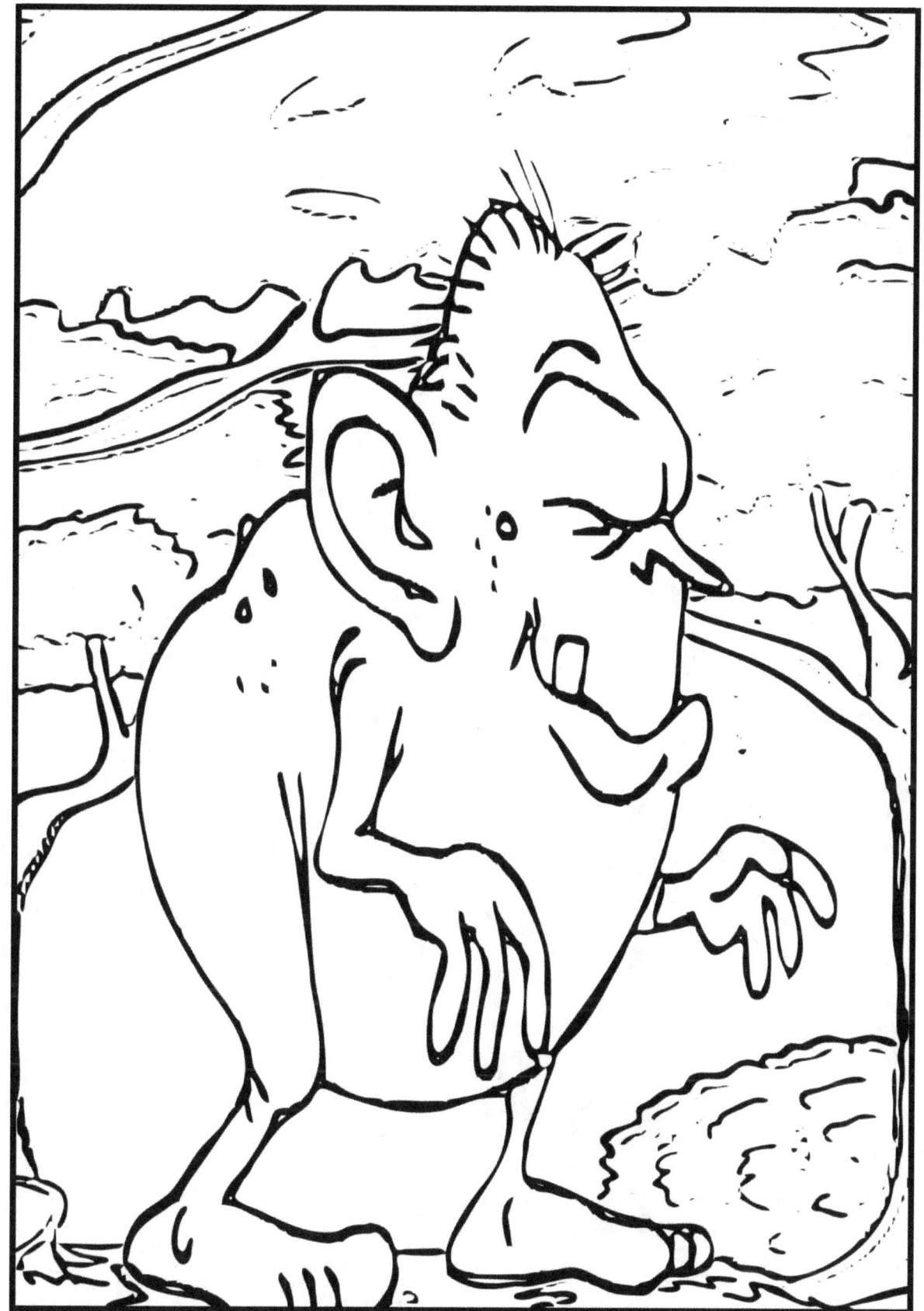

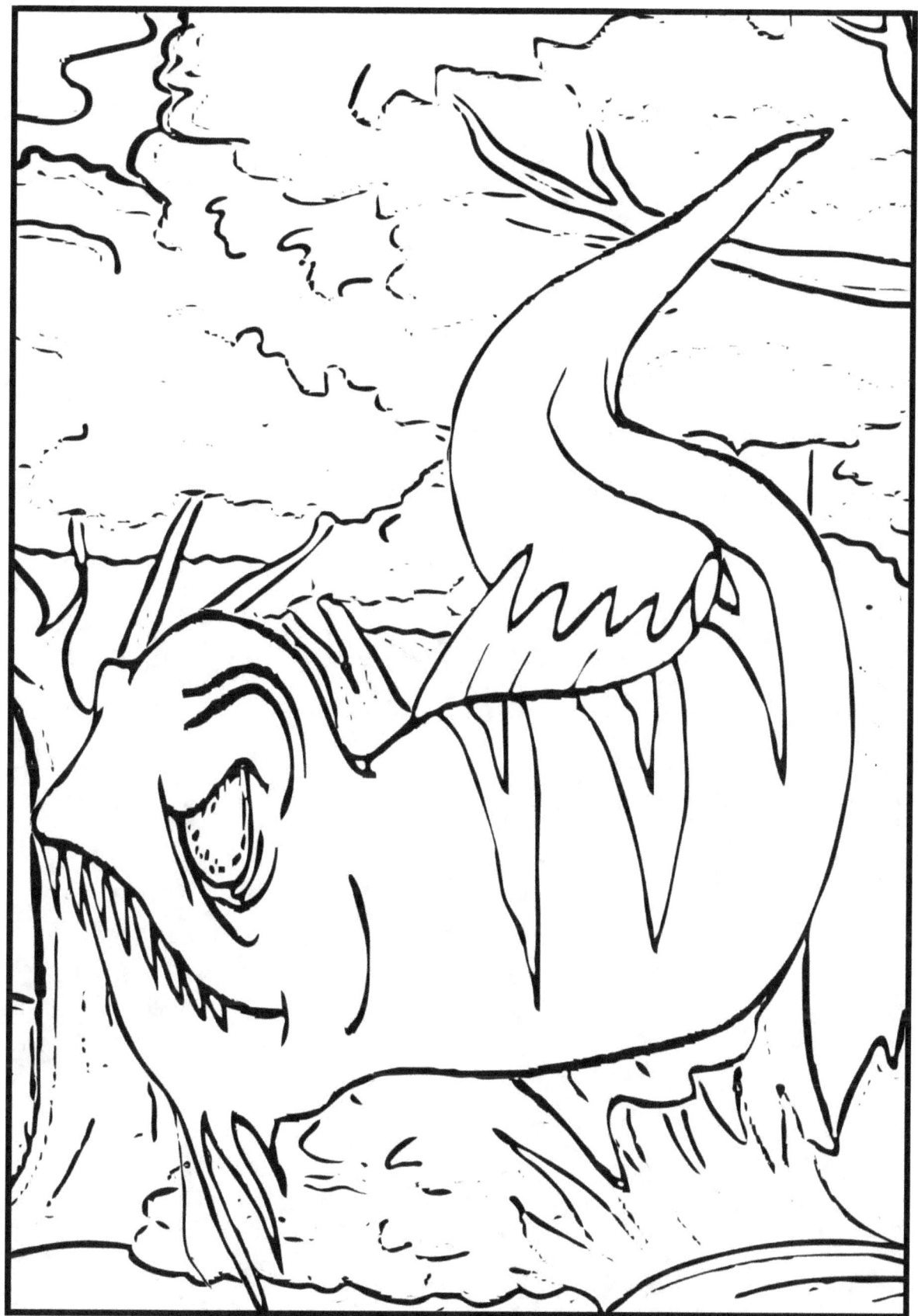

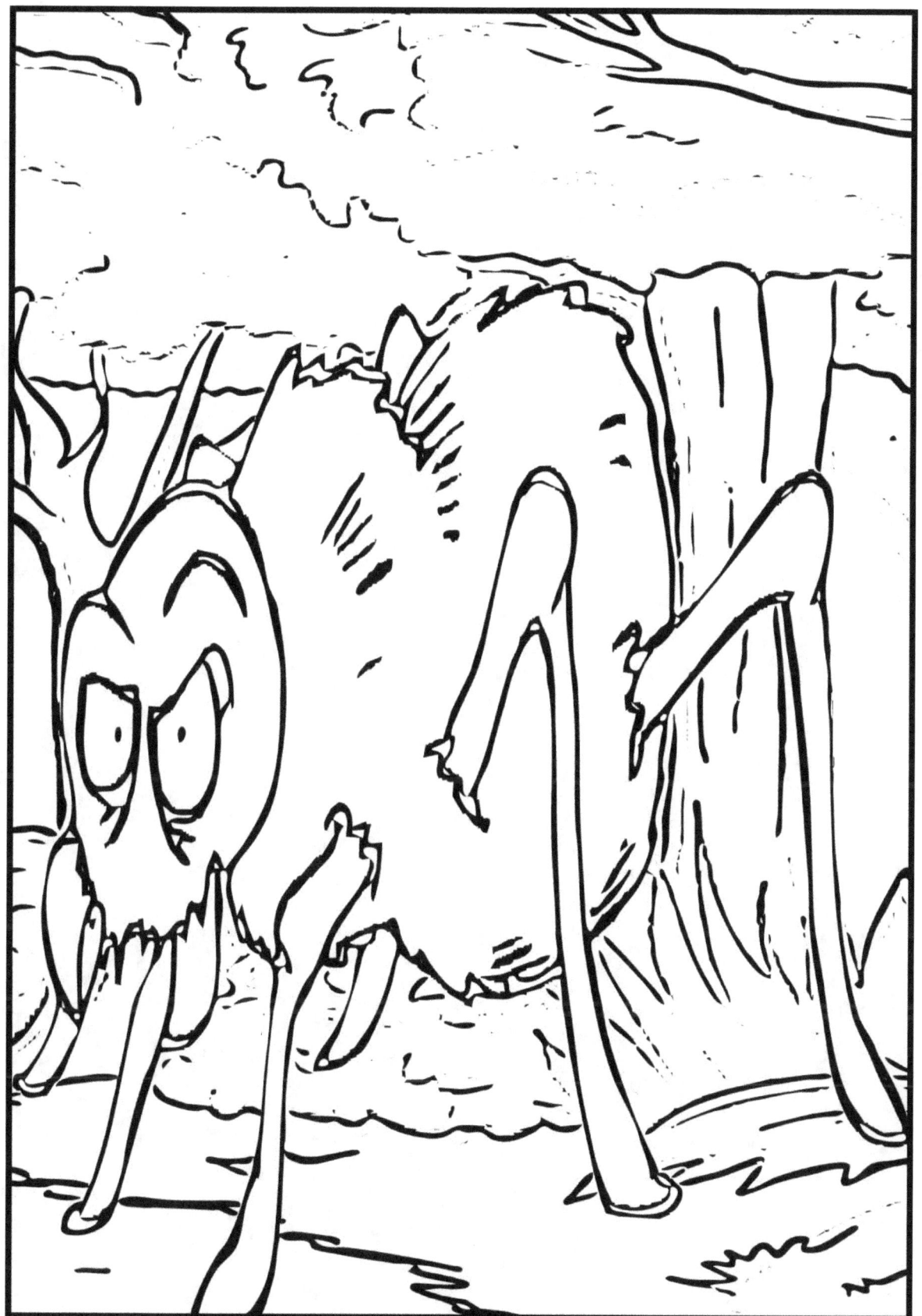

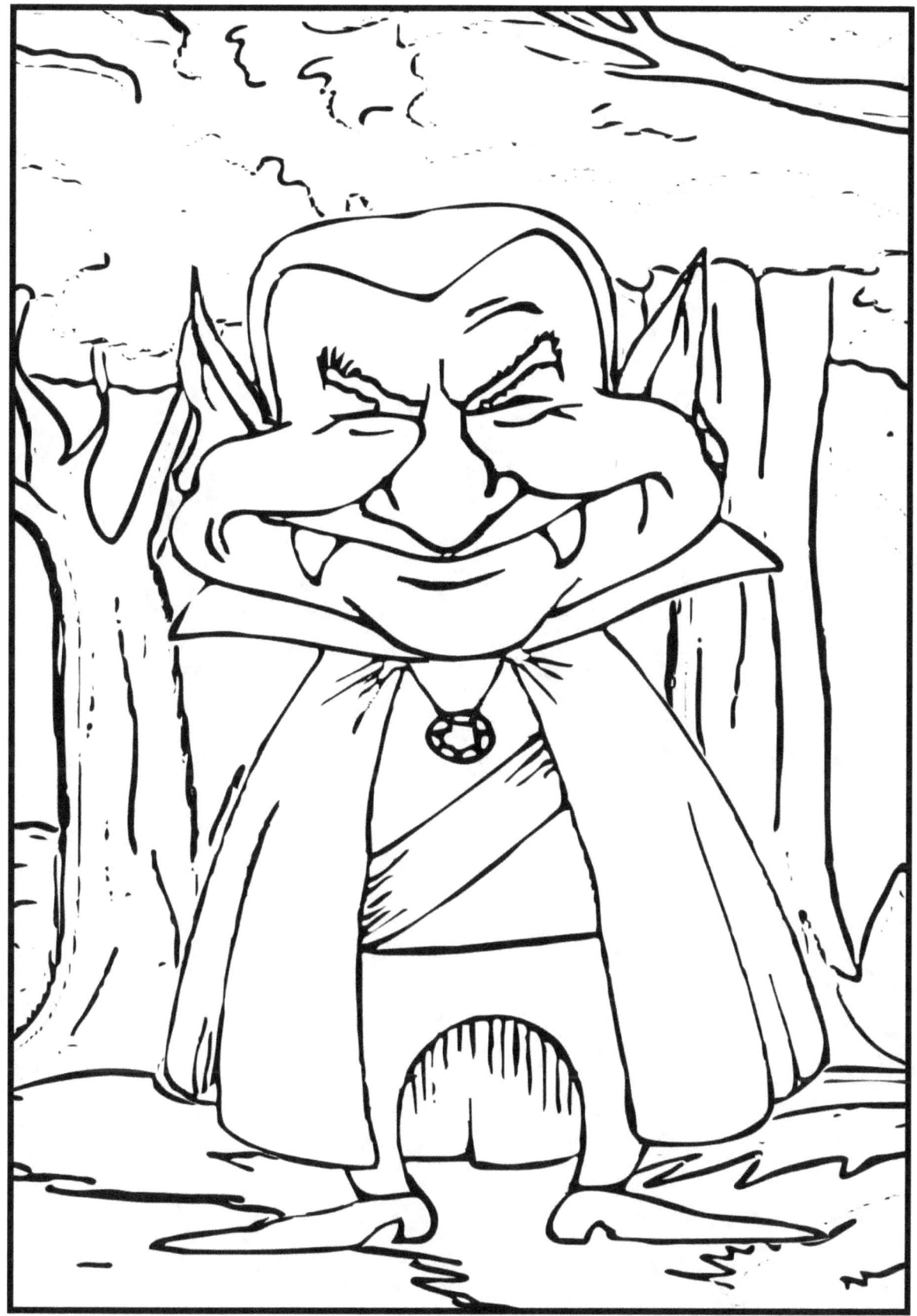

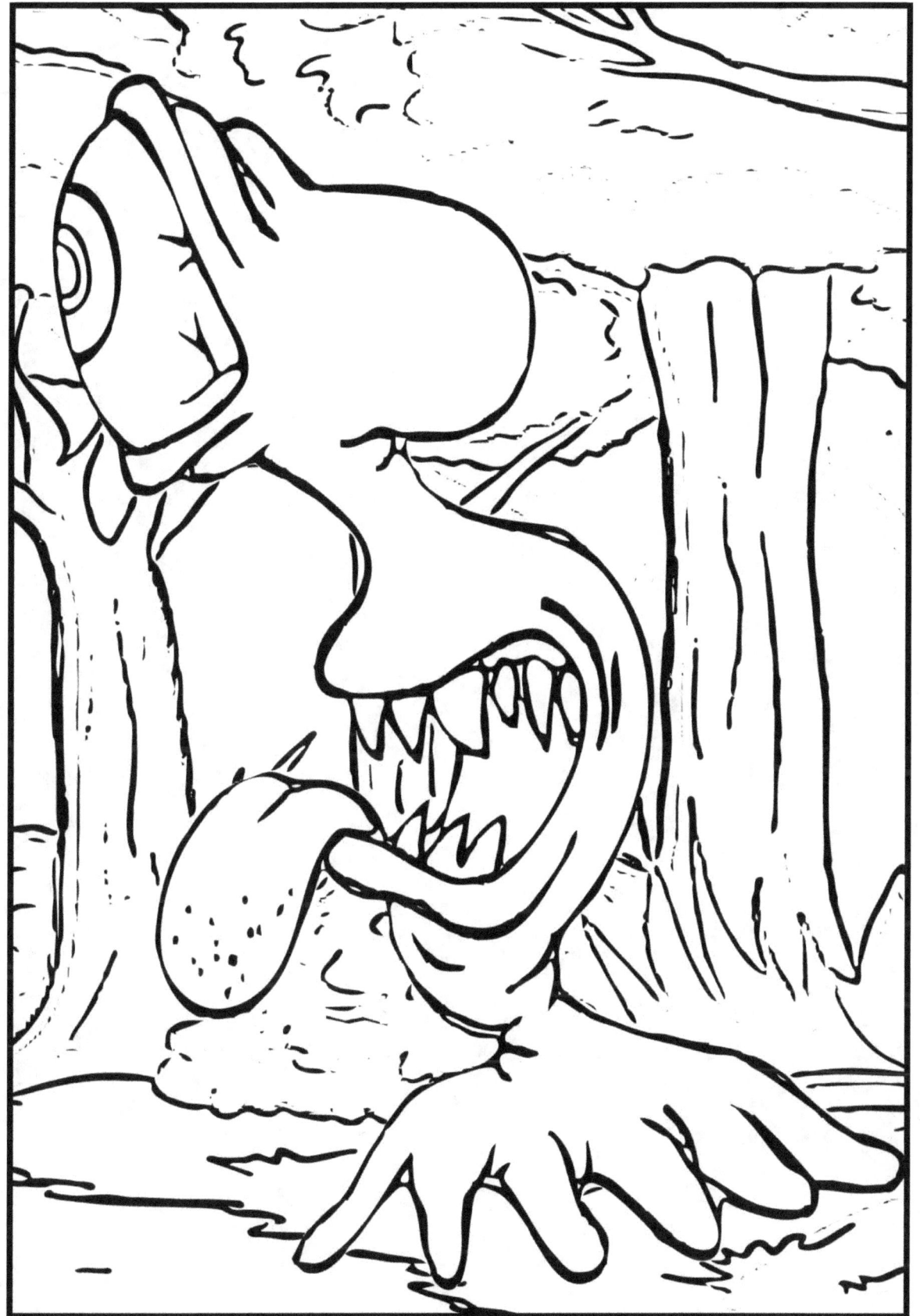

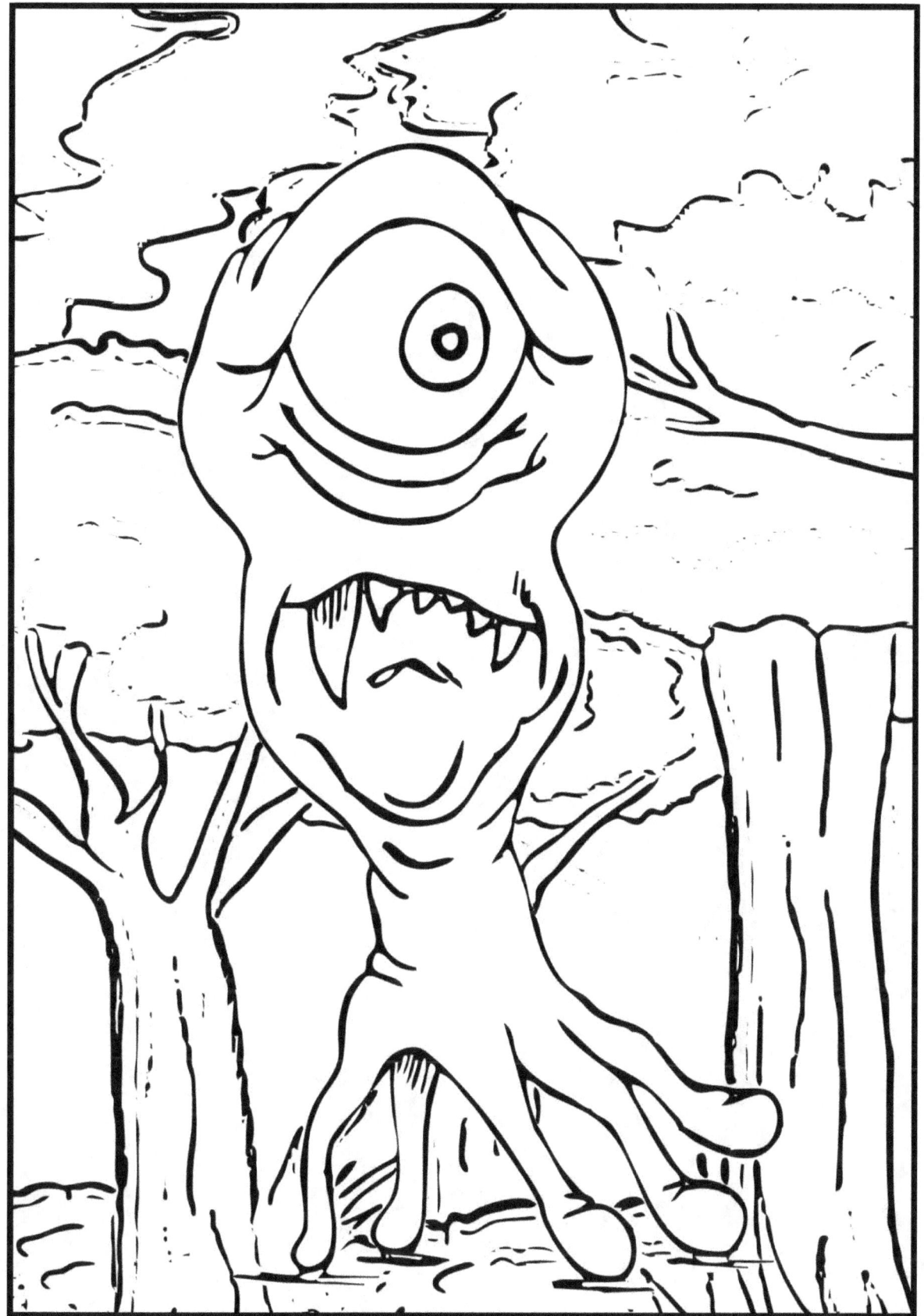

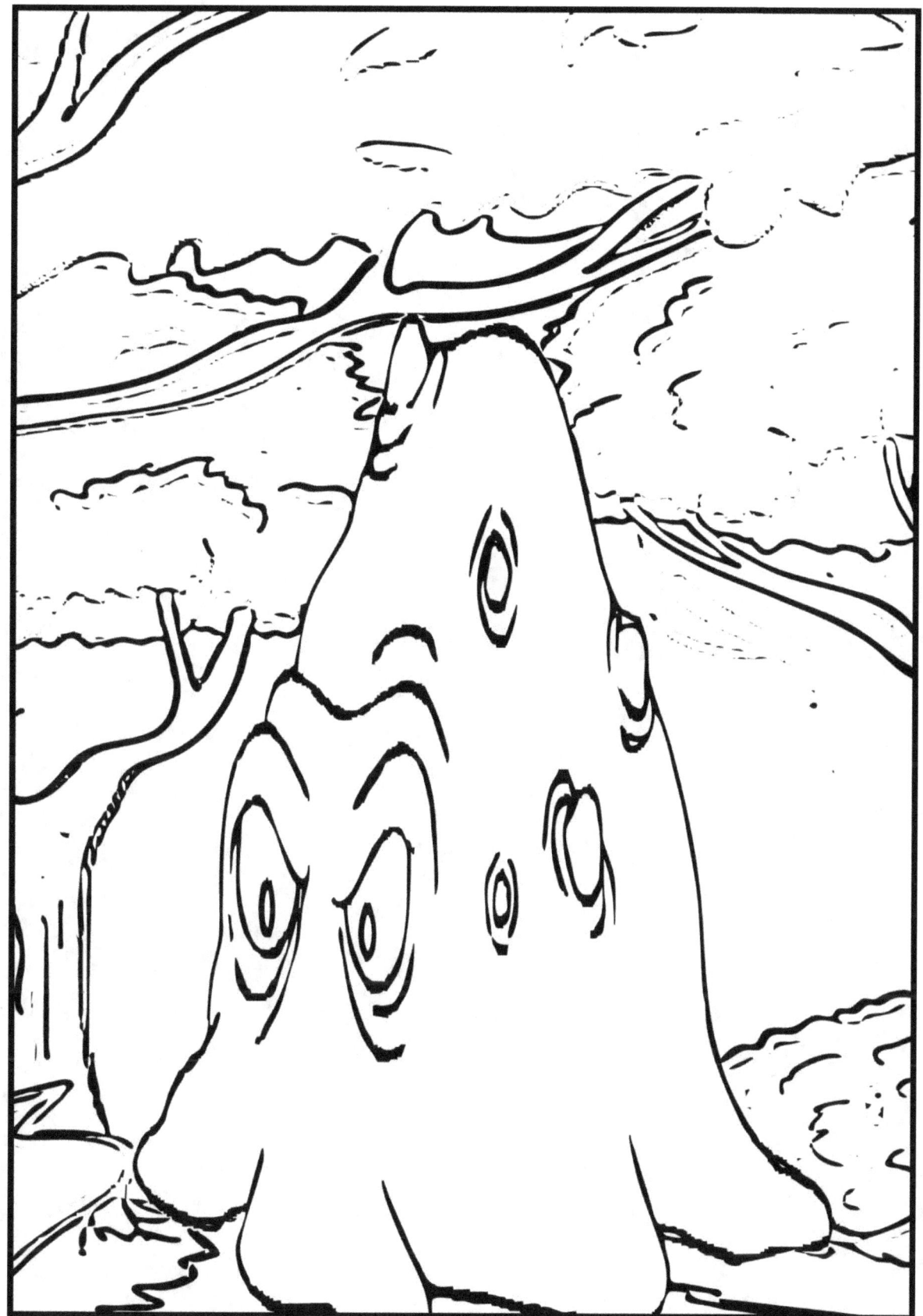

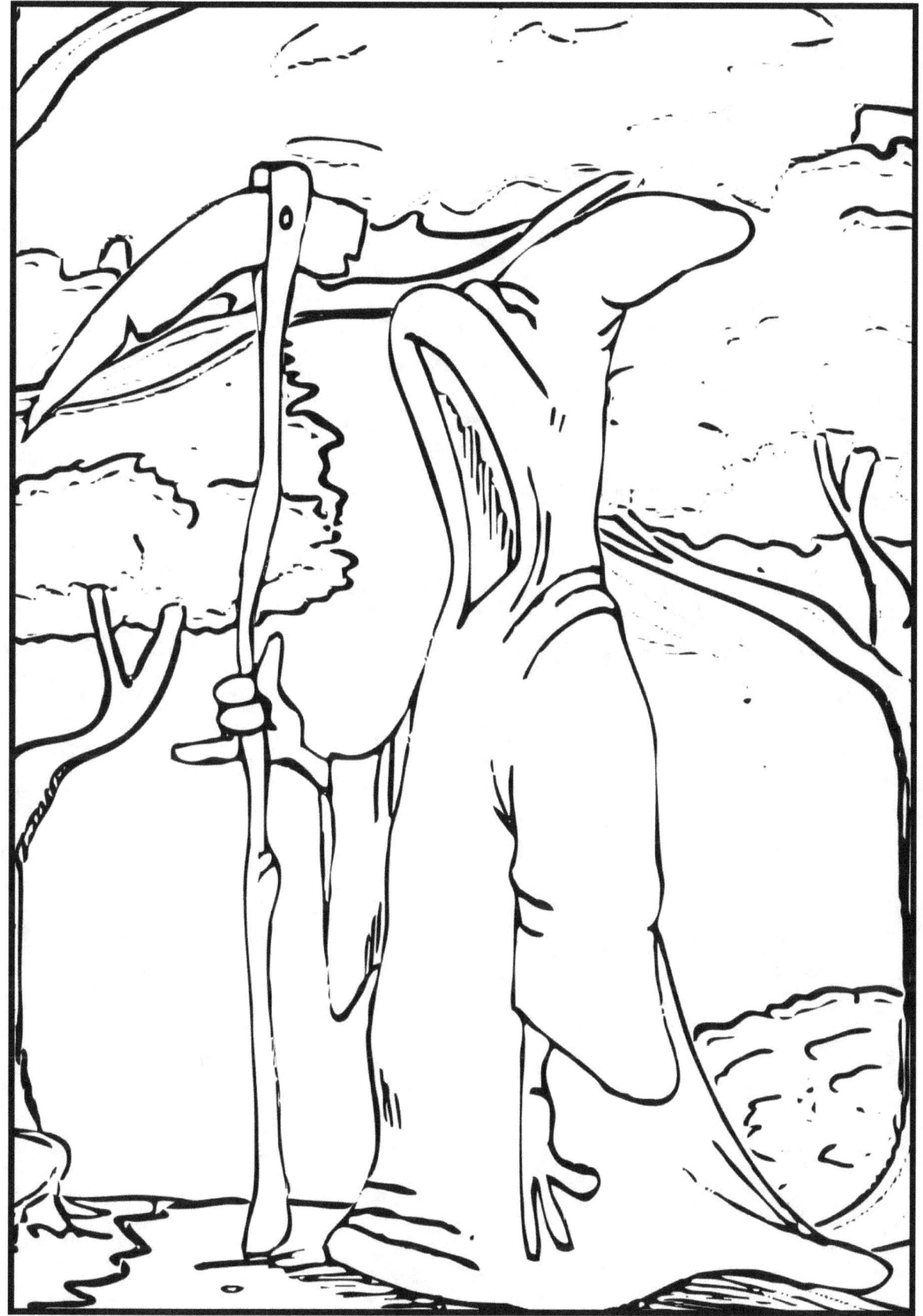

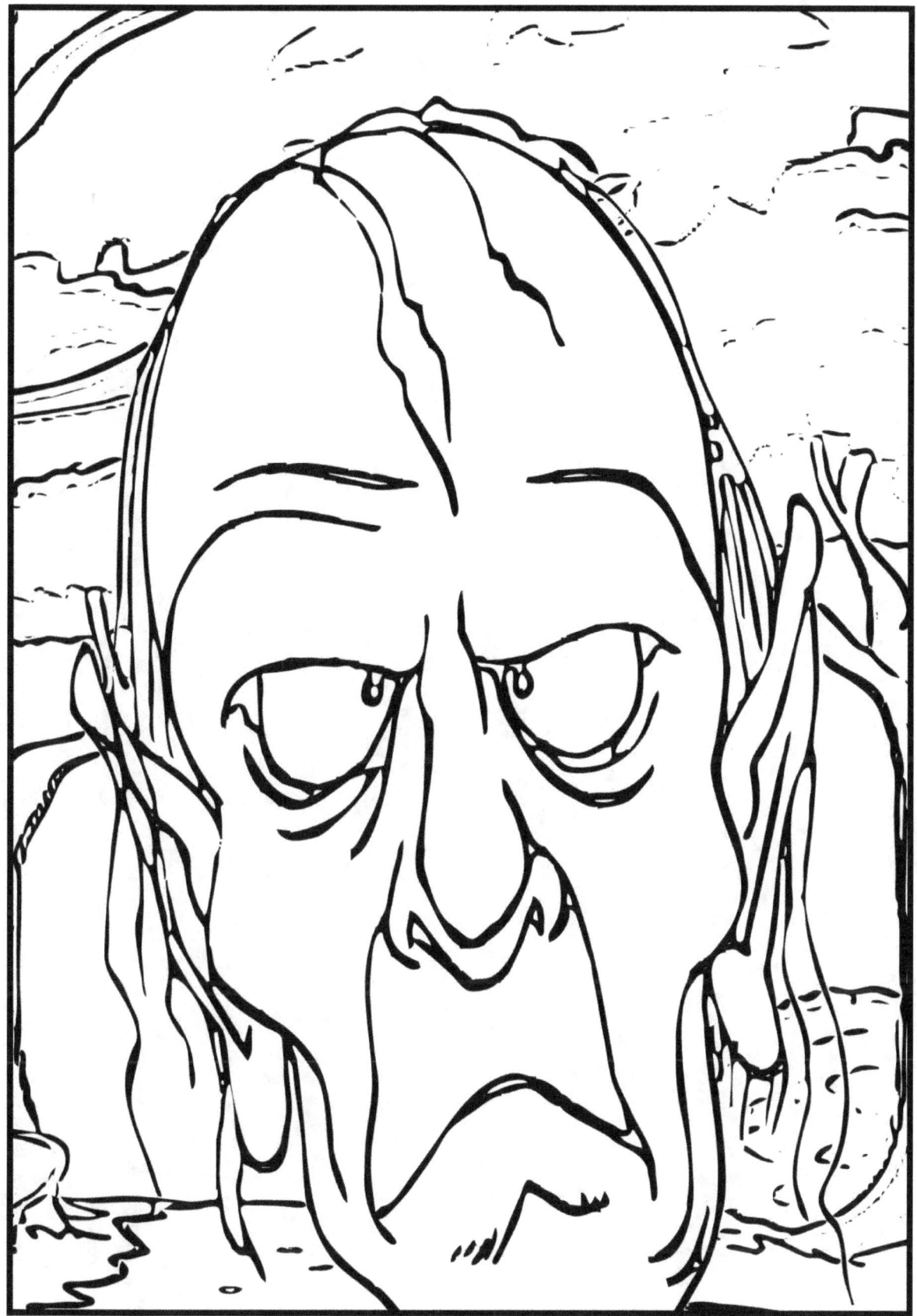

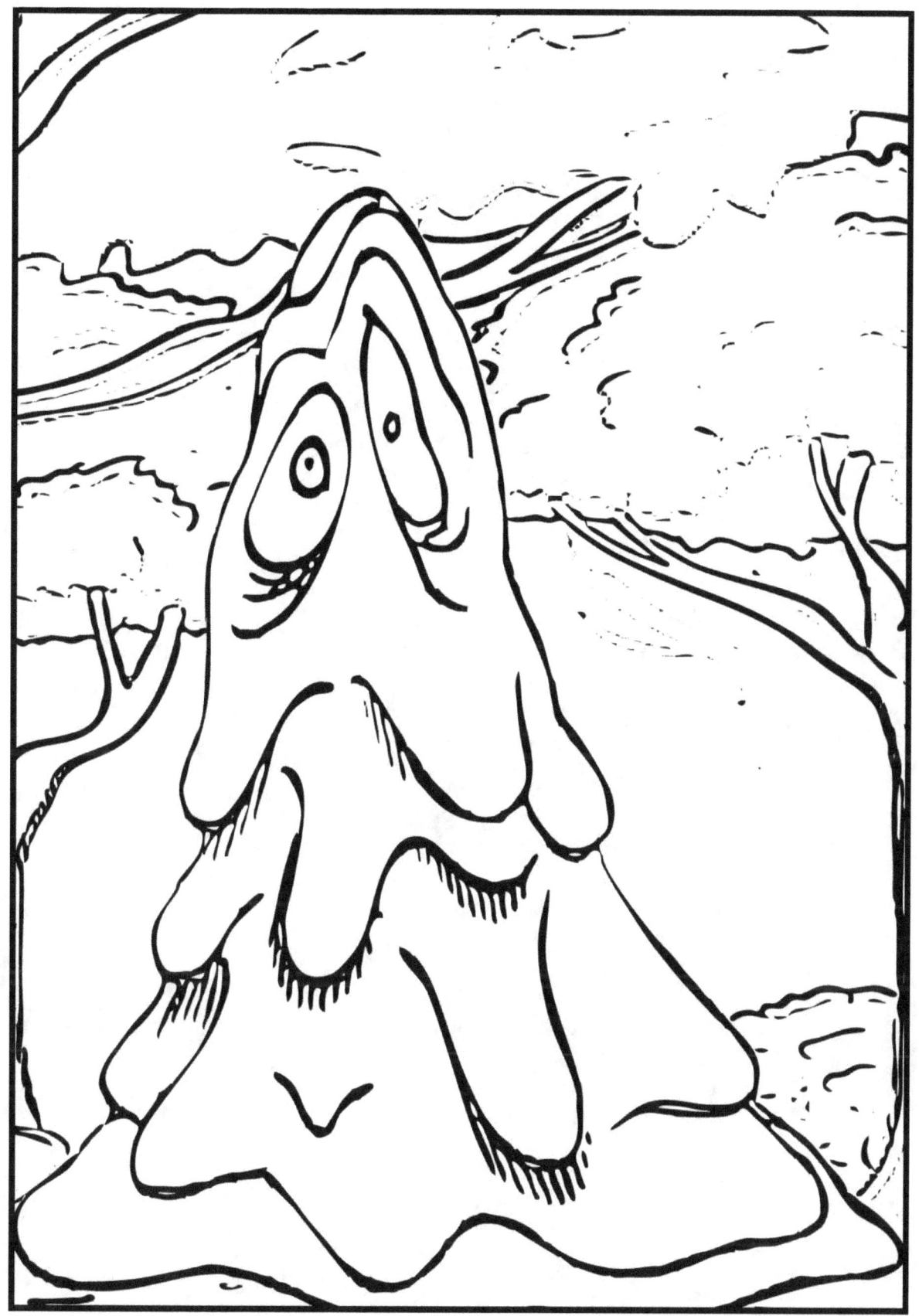

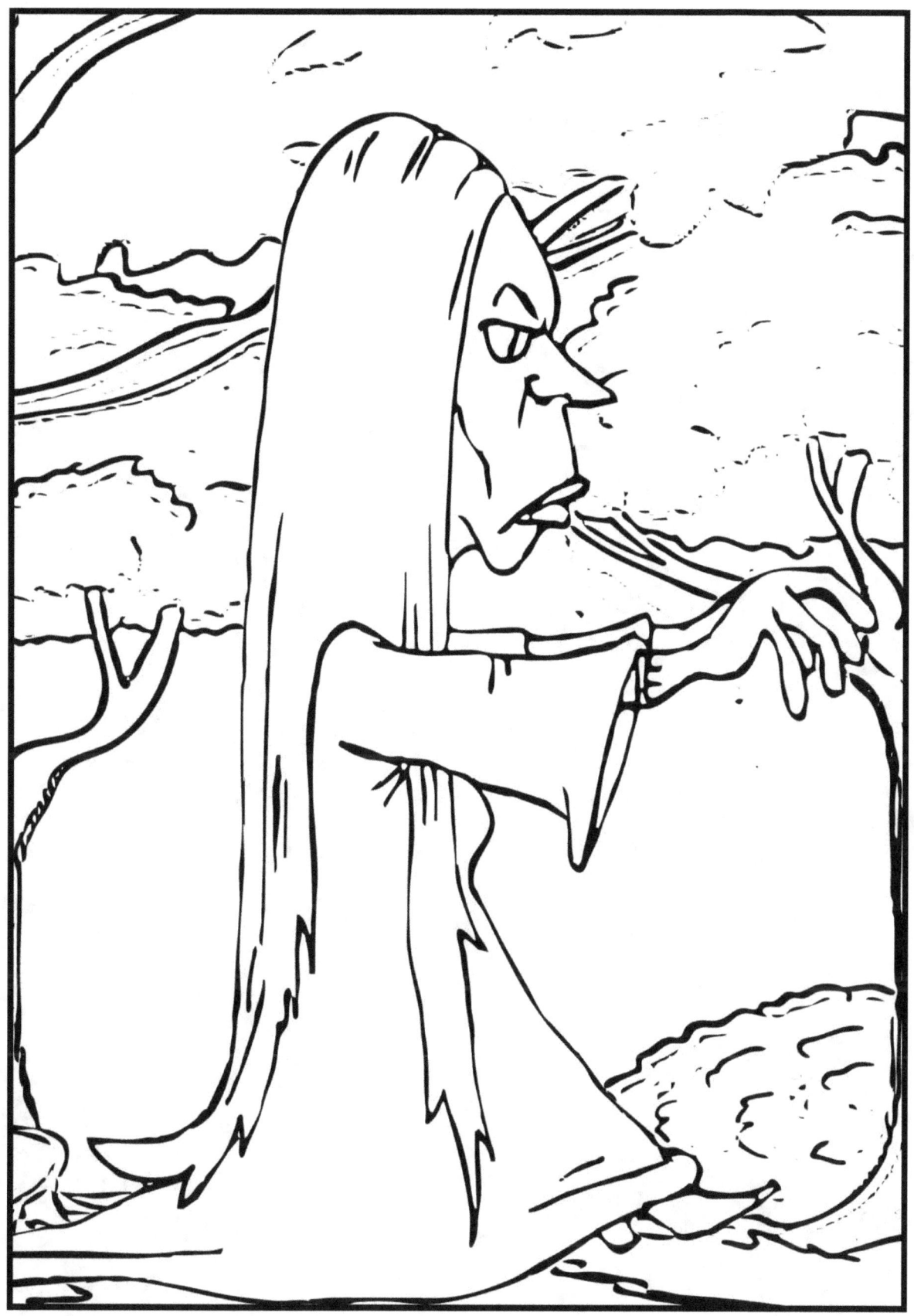

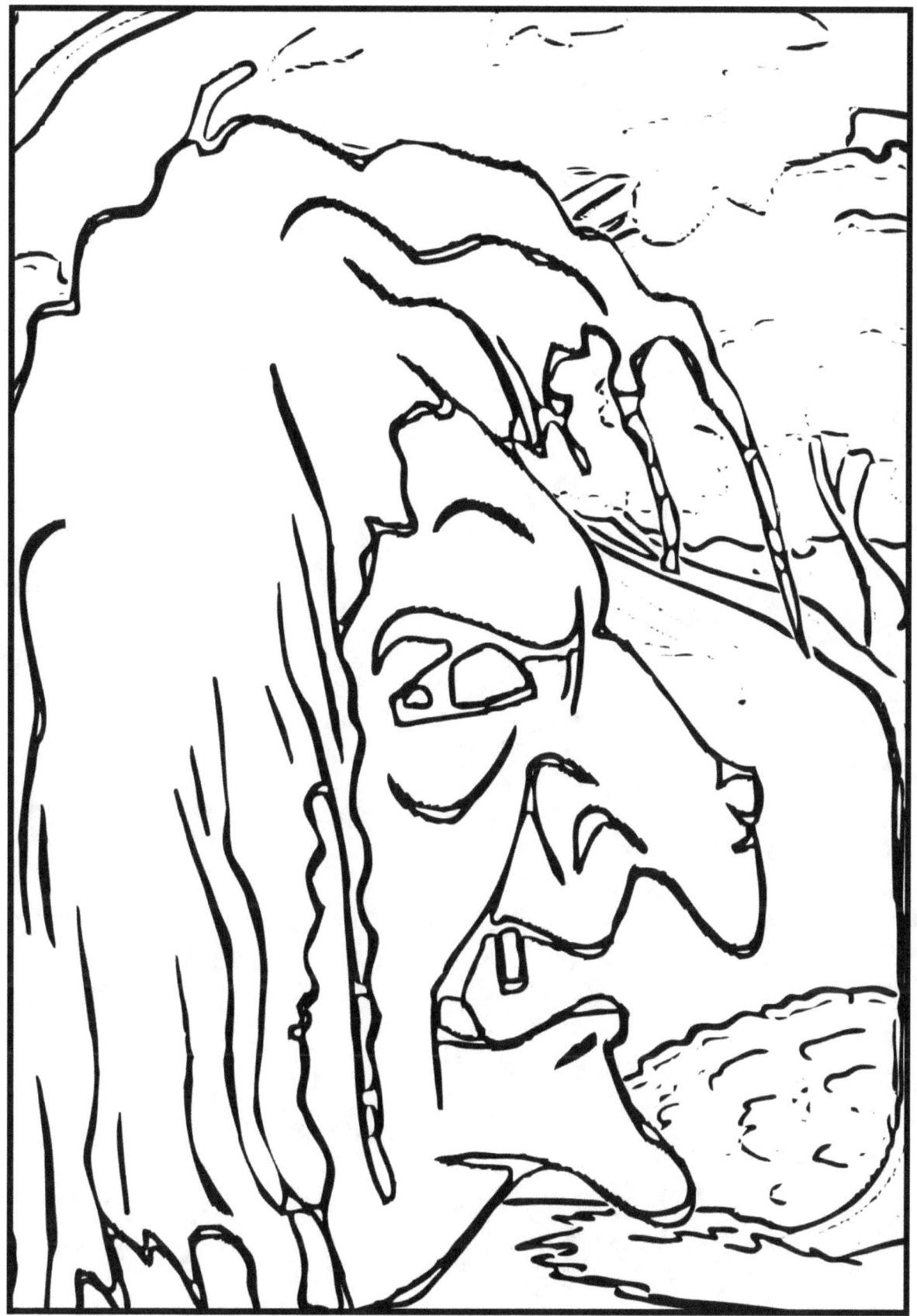

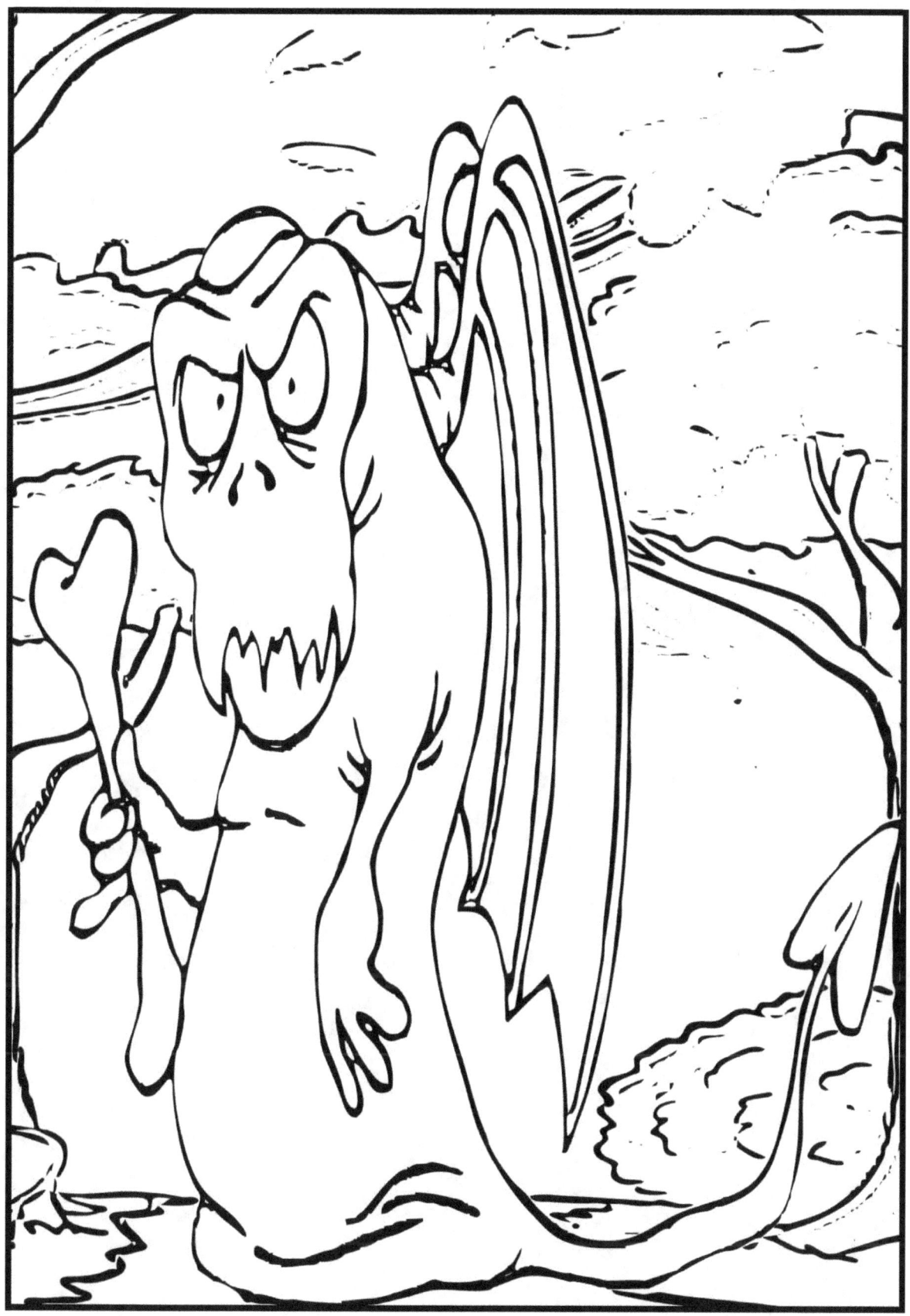

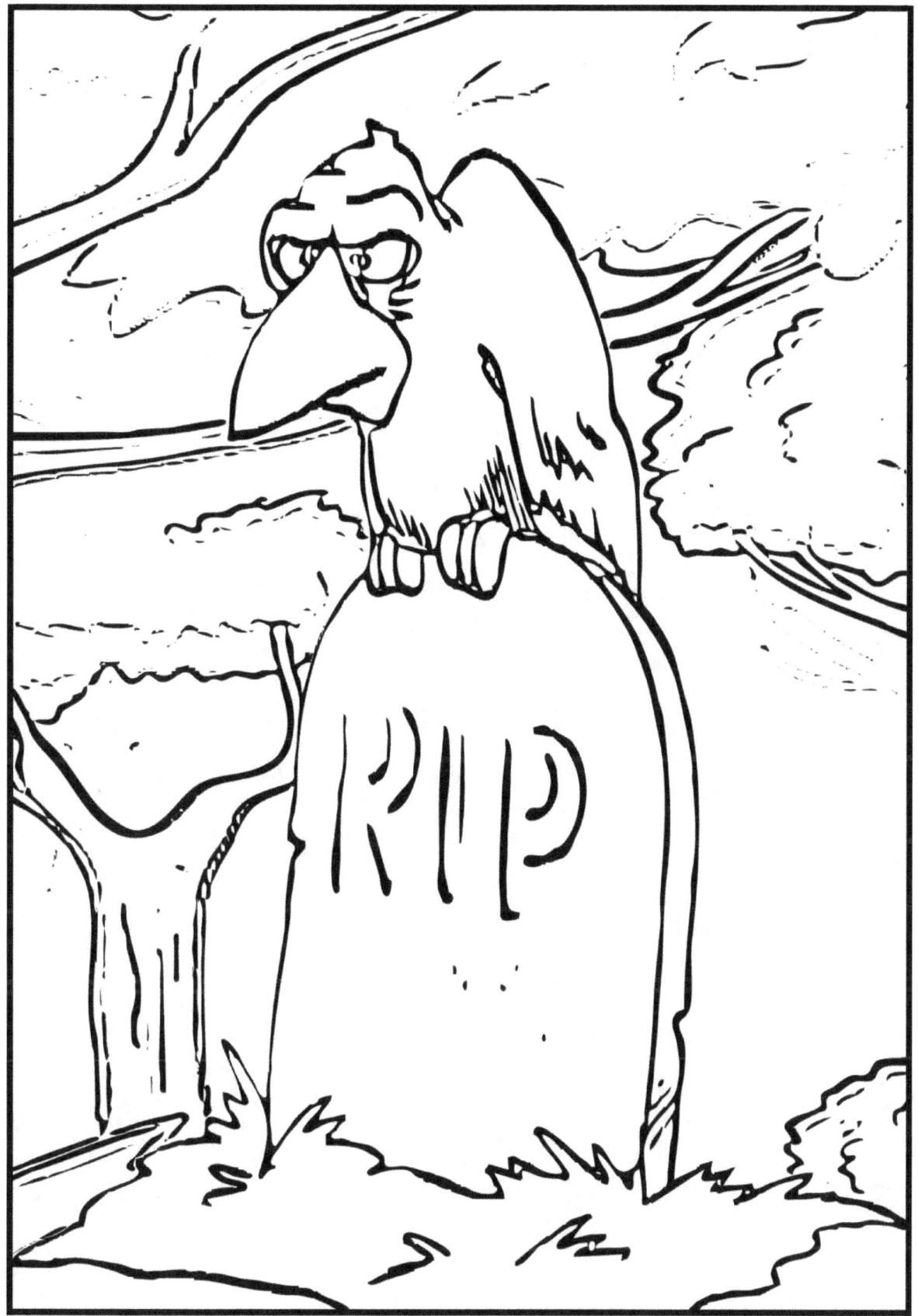

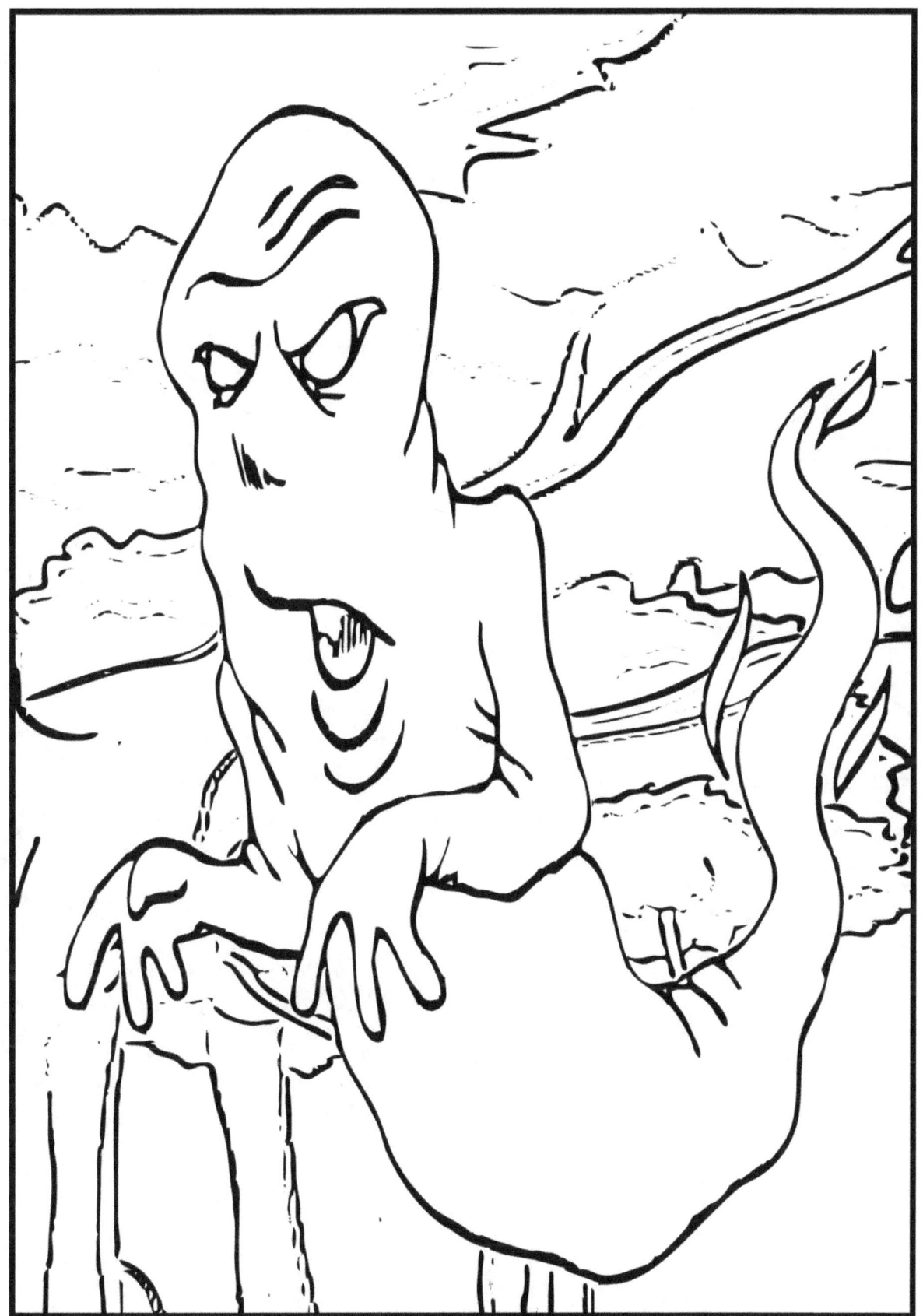

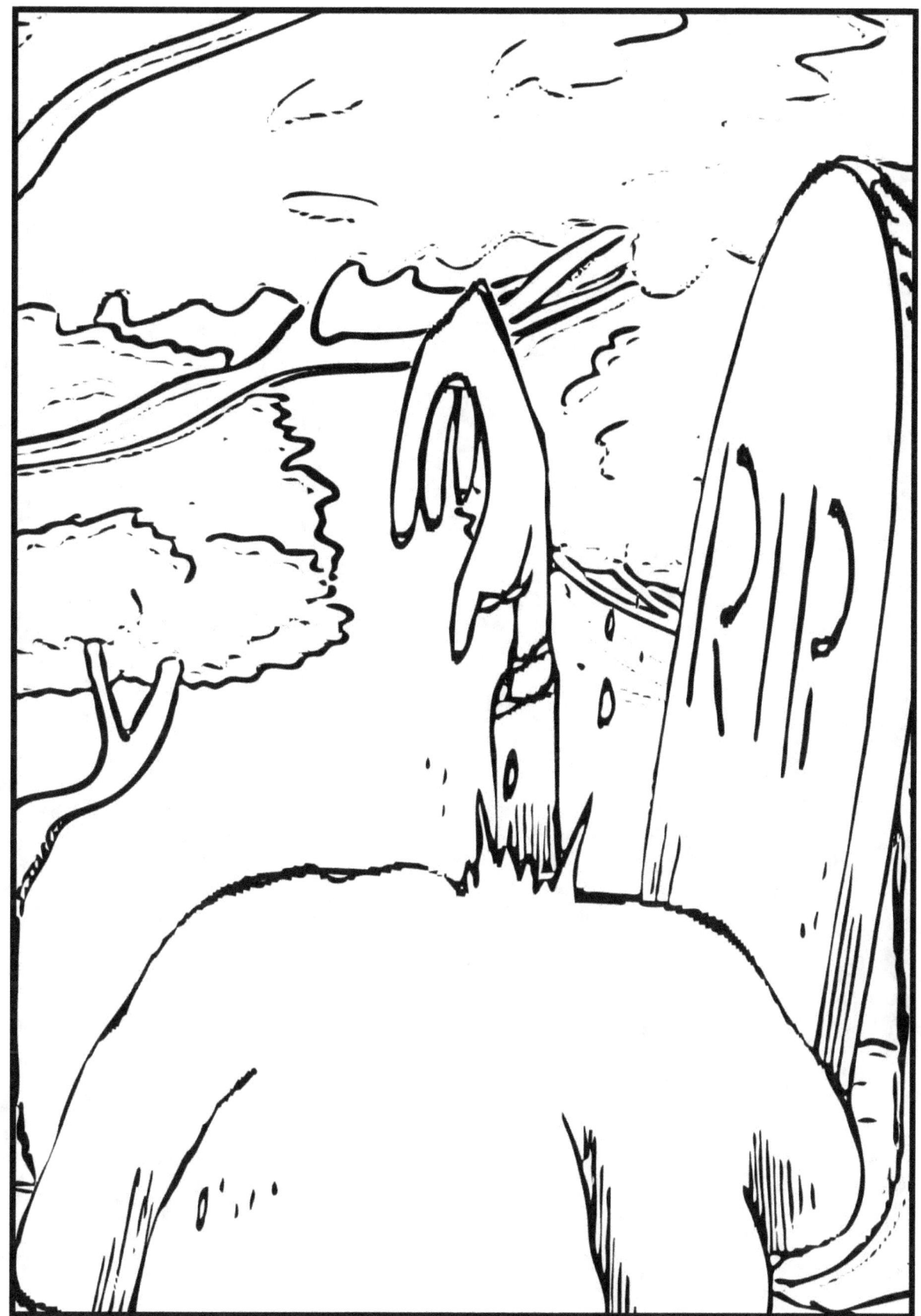

POPULAR TALES

Coloring Book

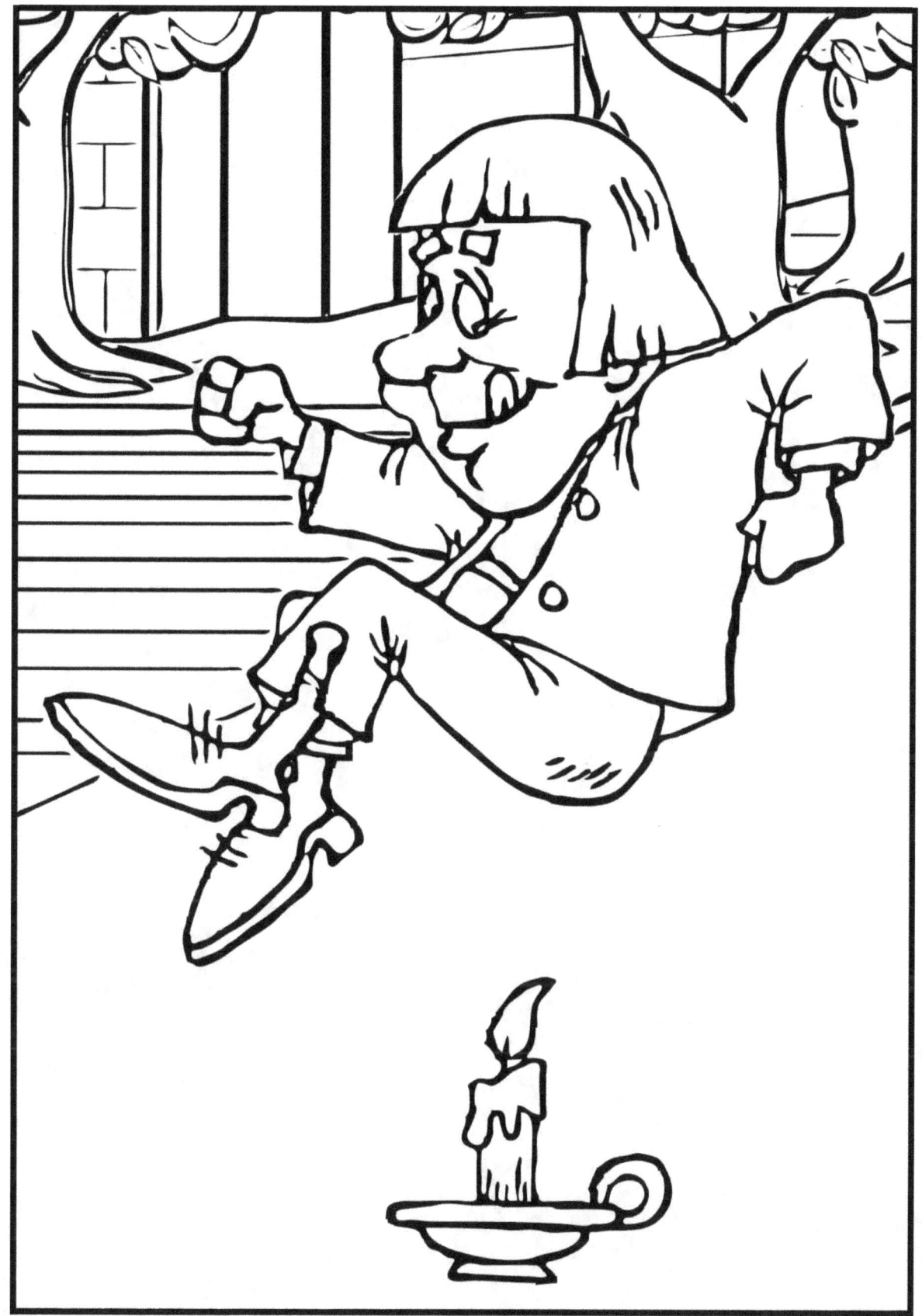

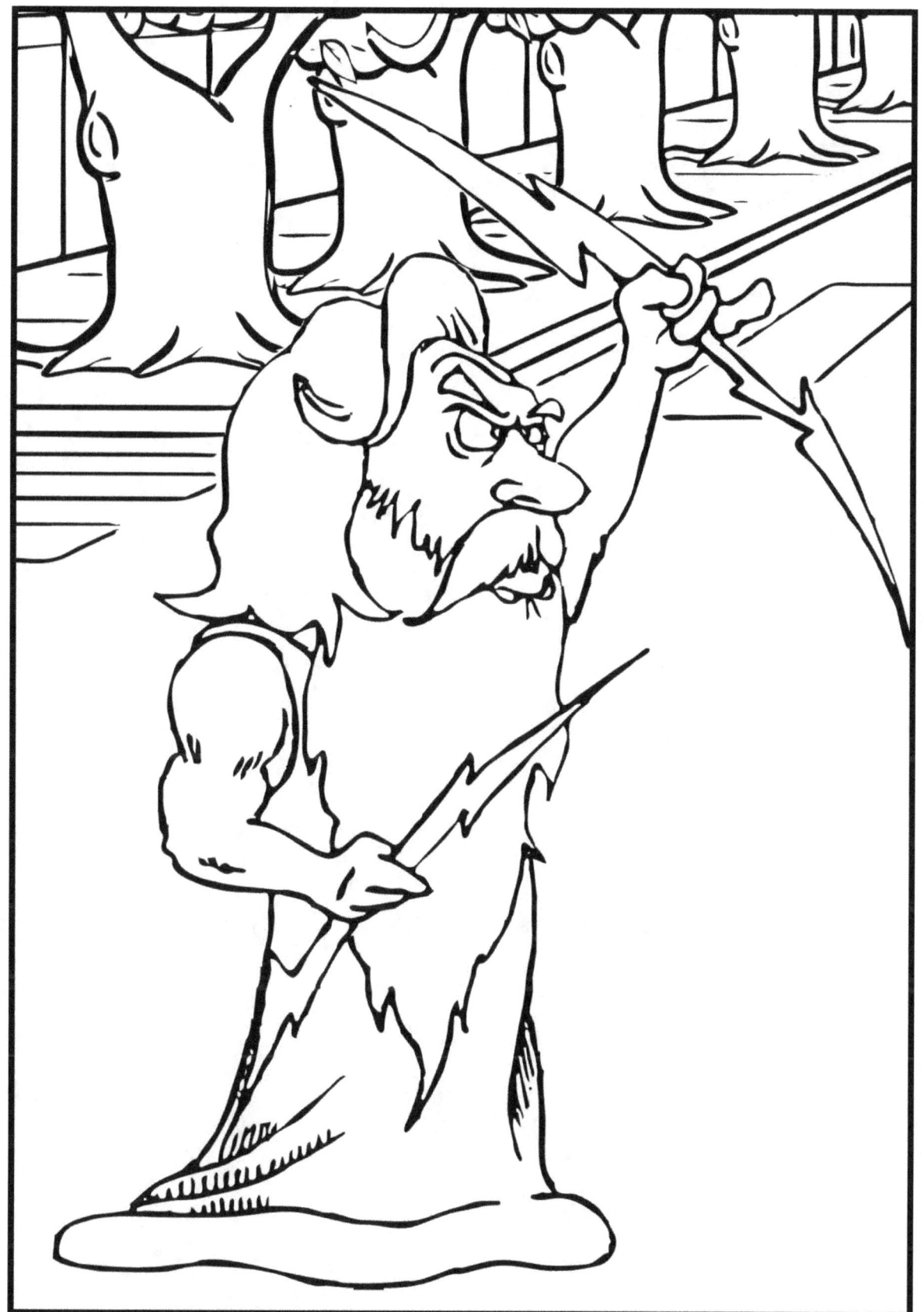

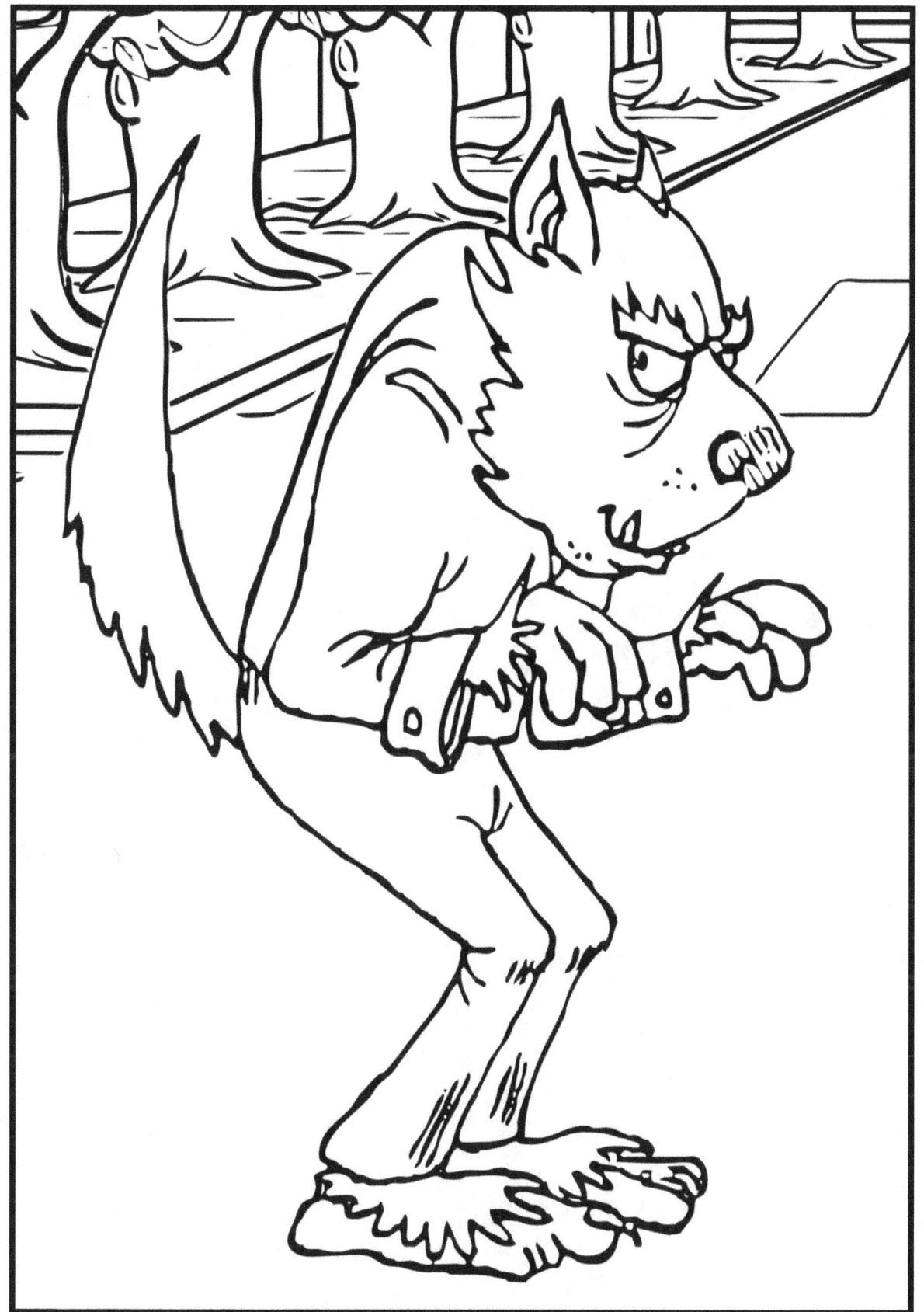

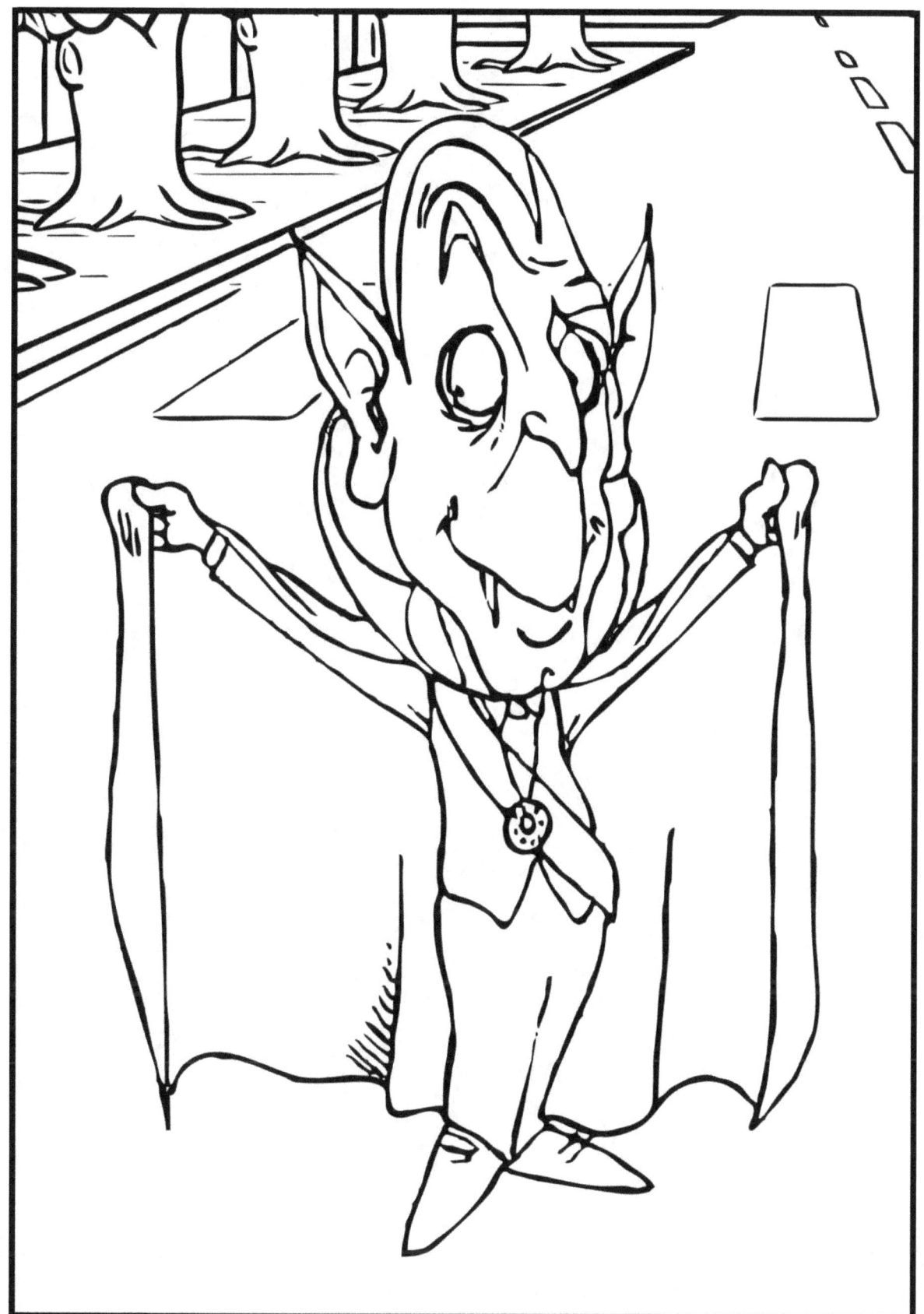

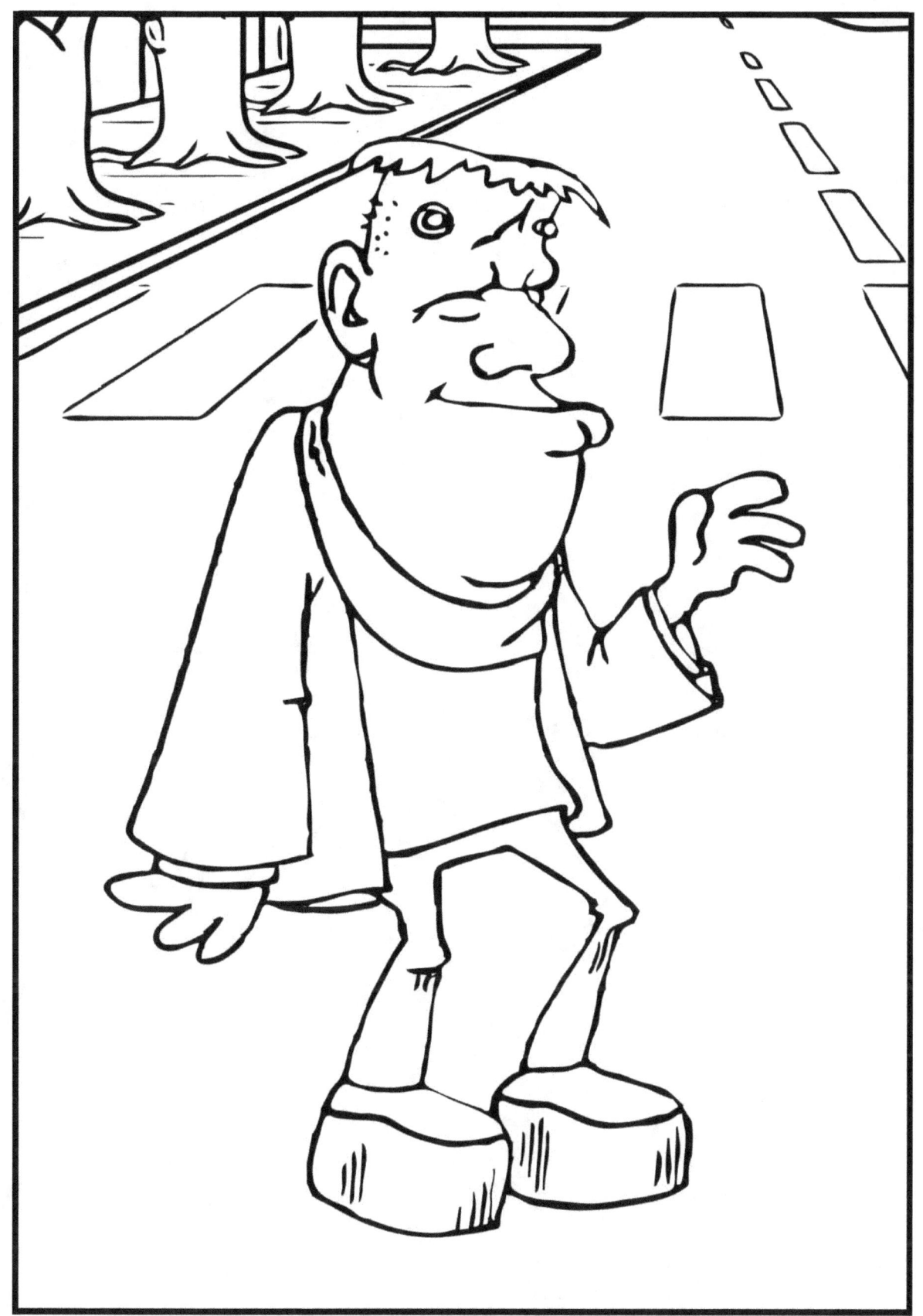

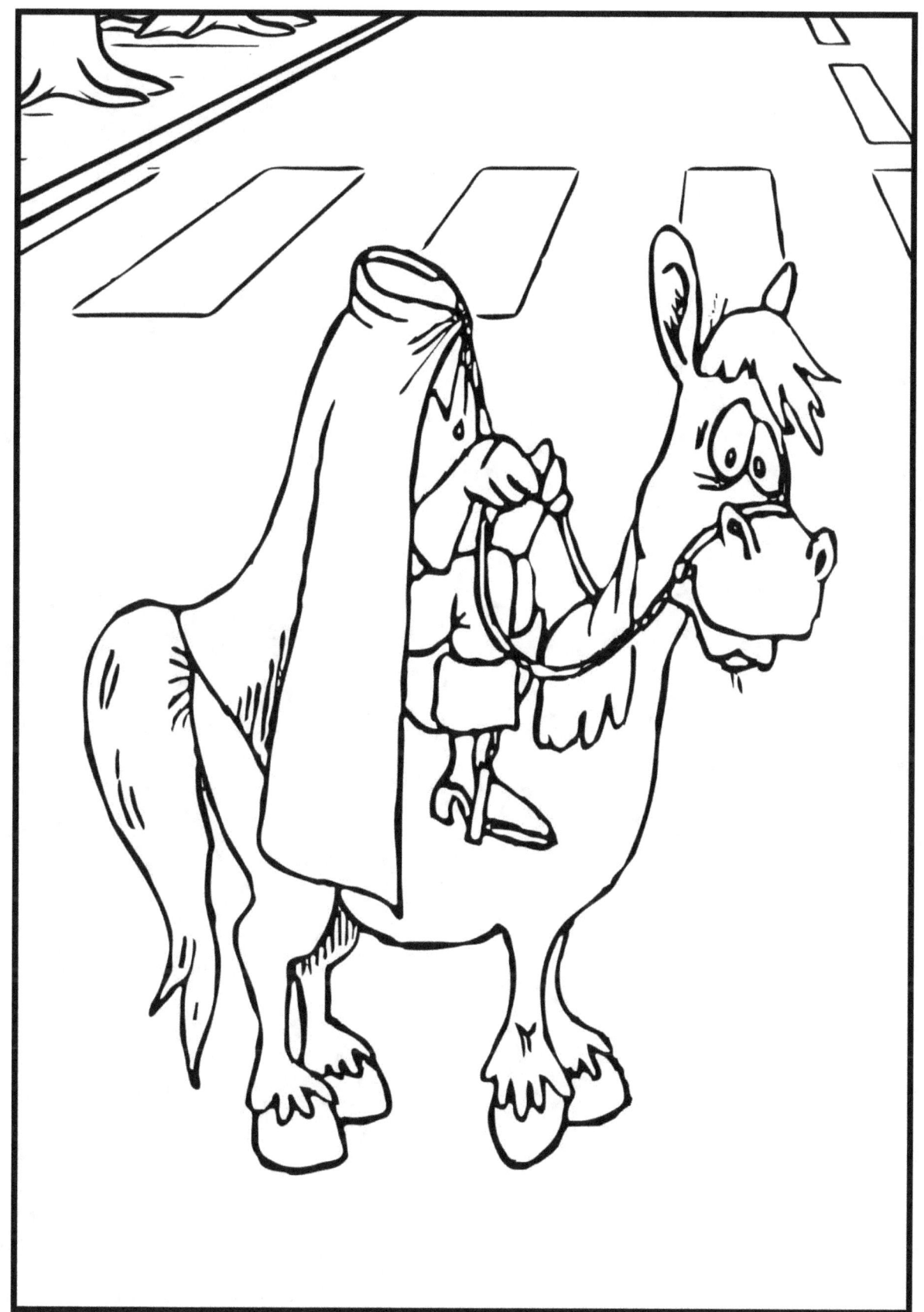

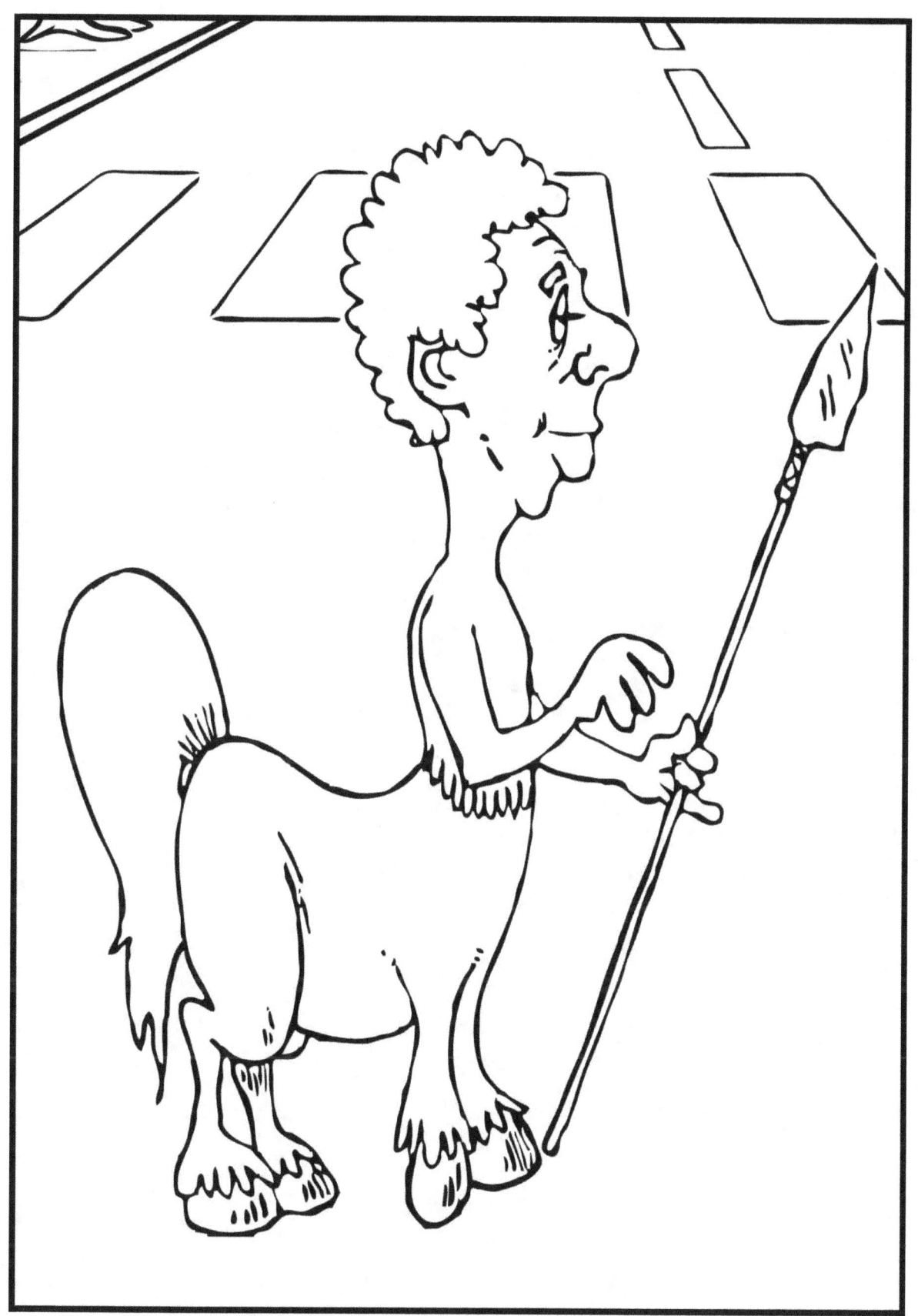

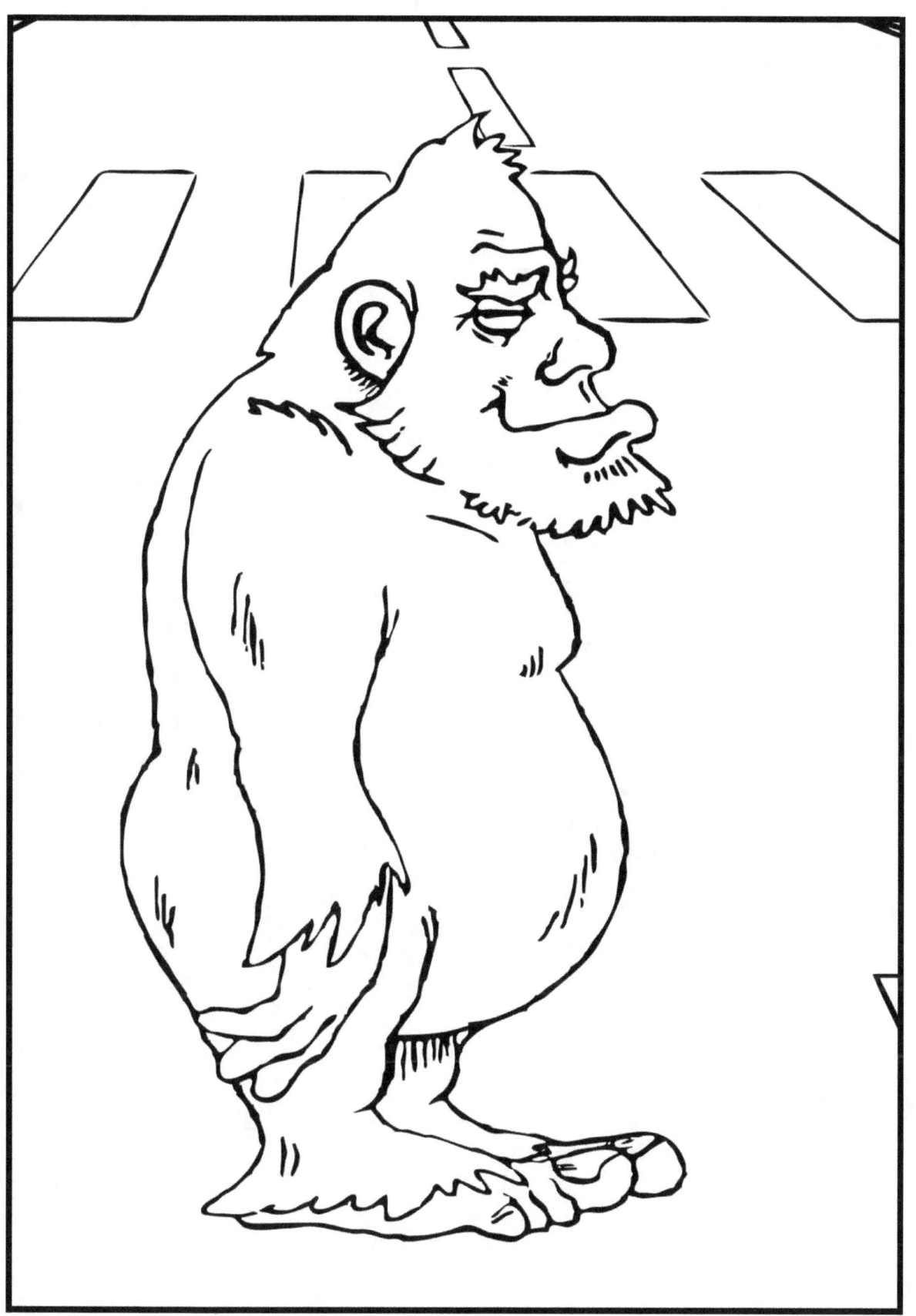

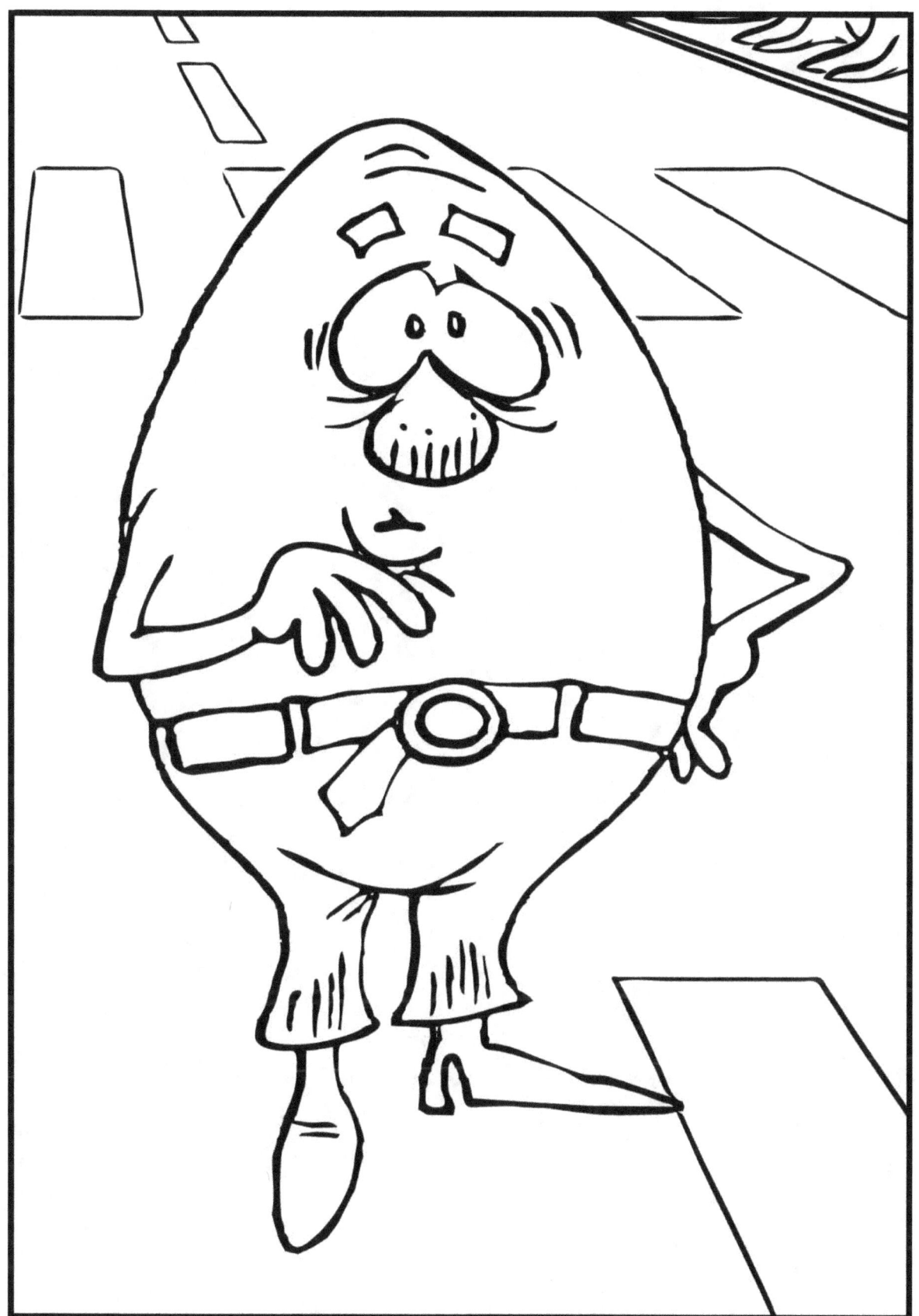

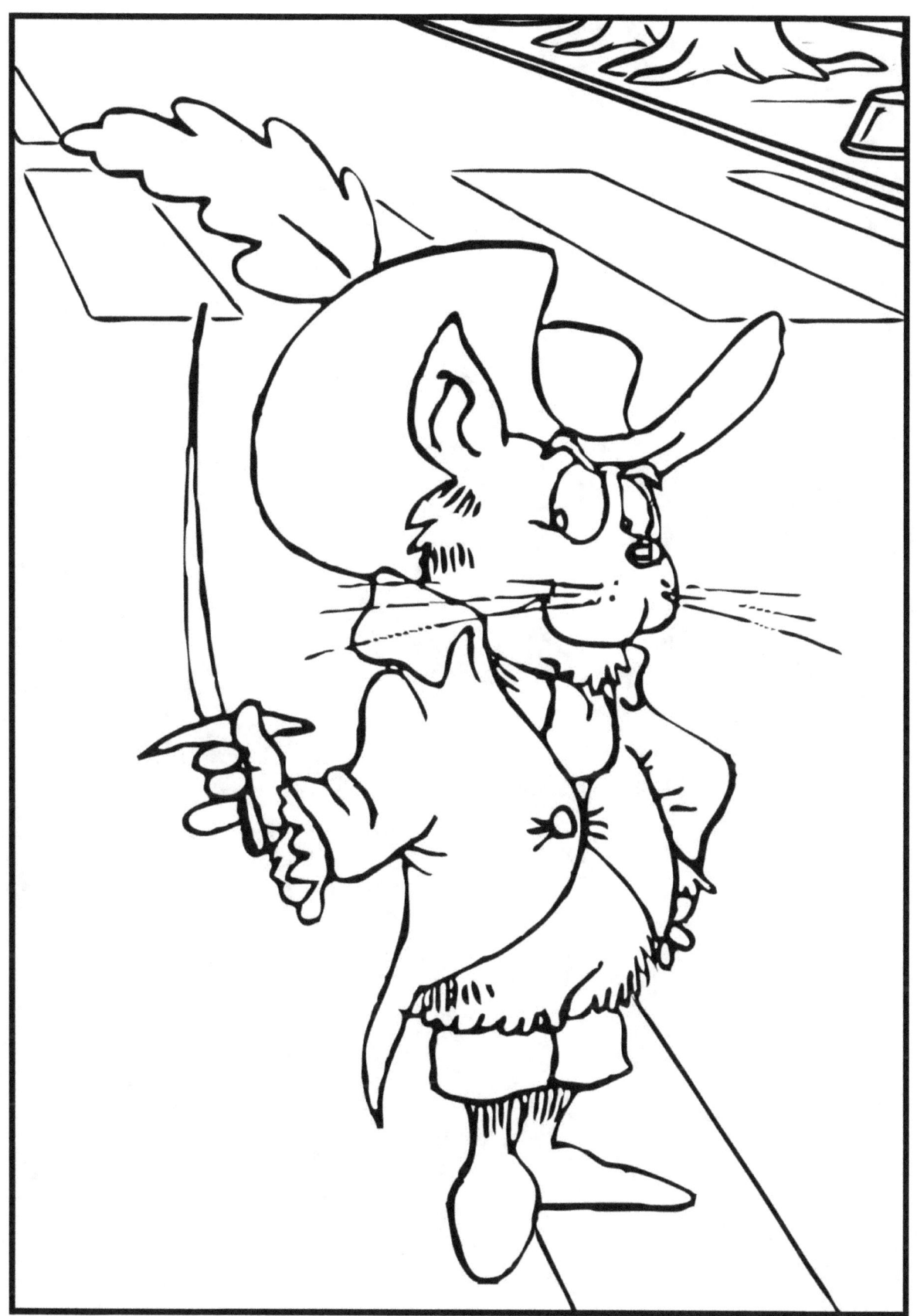

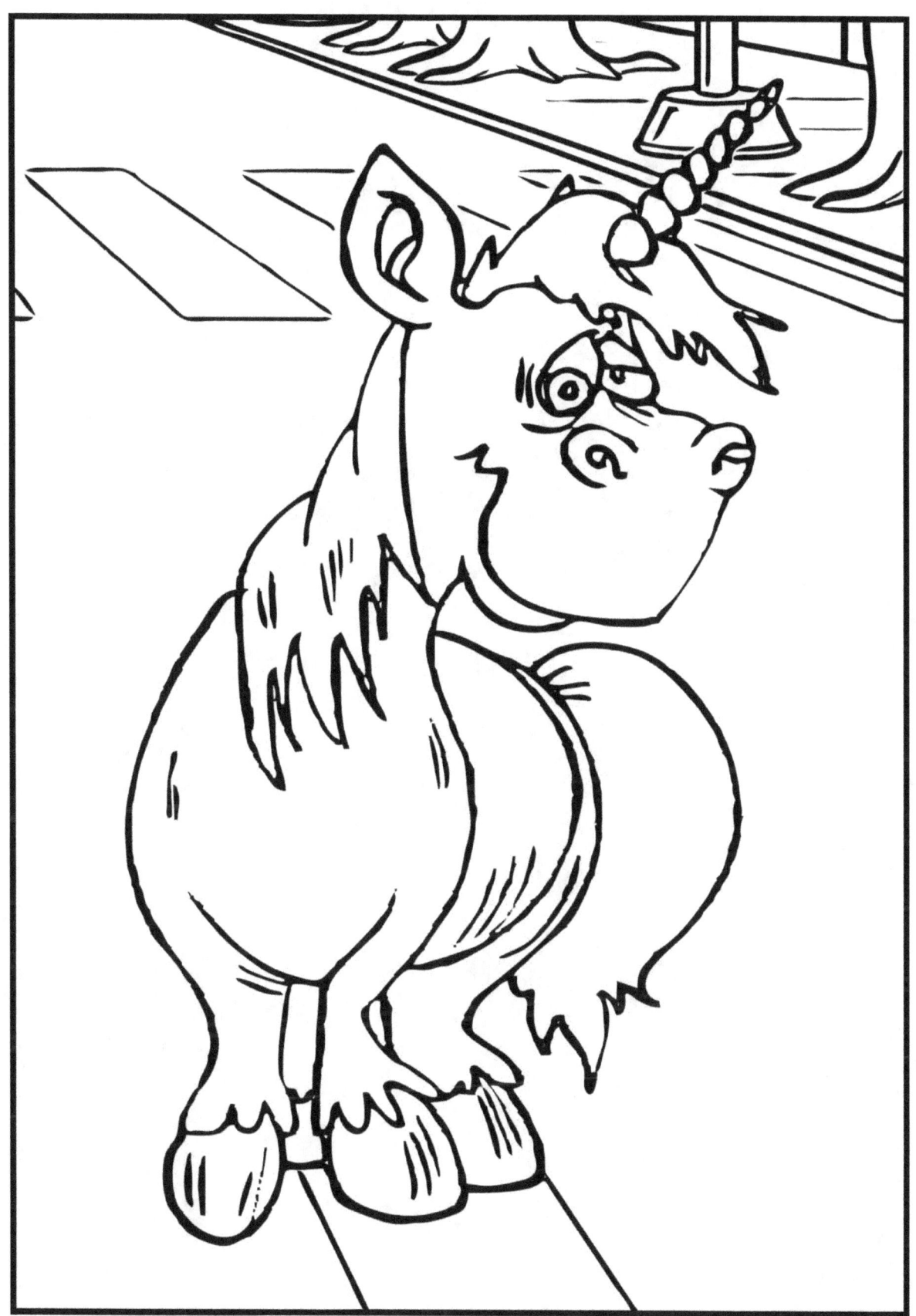

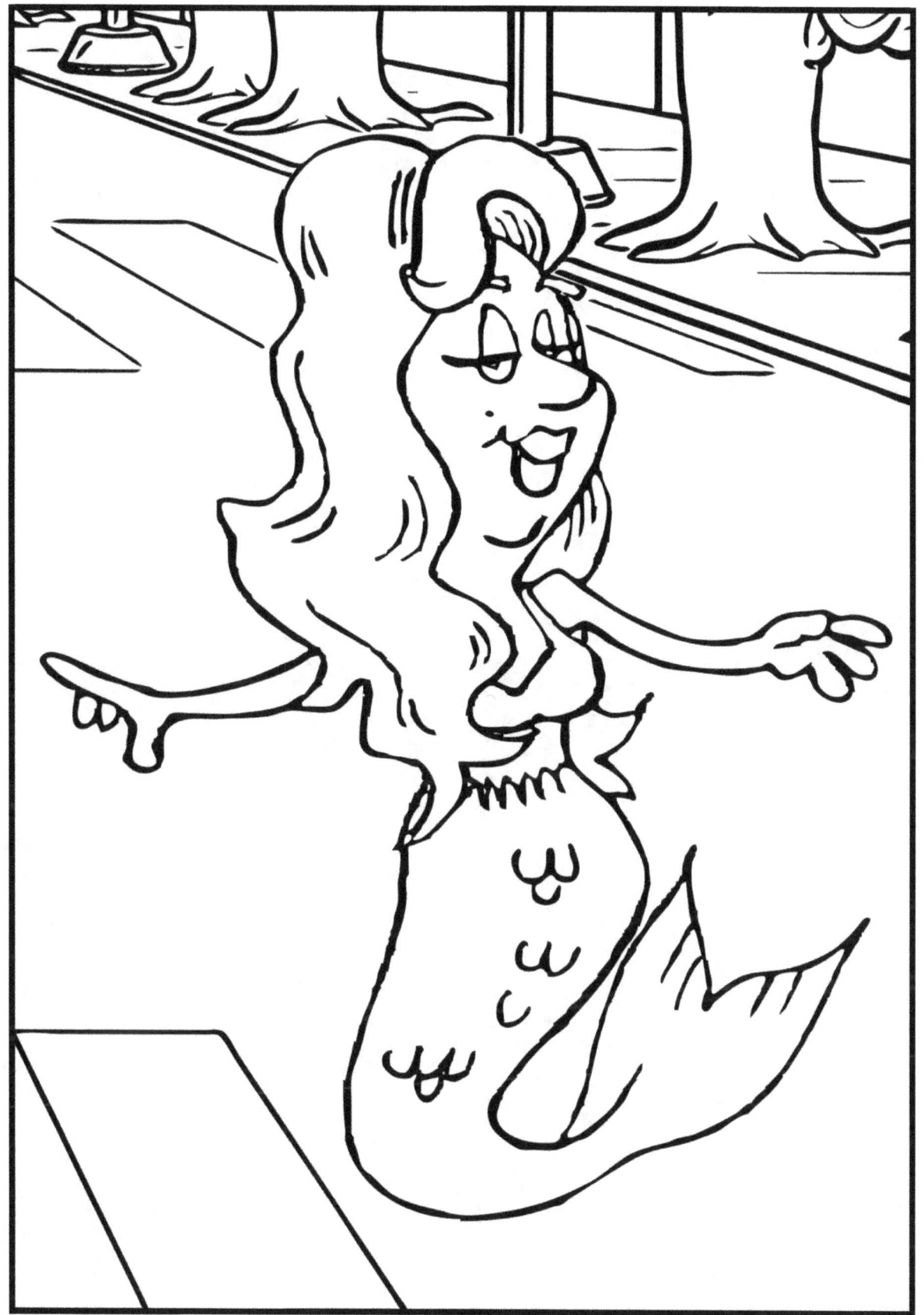

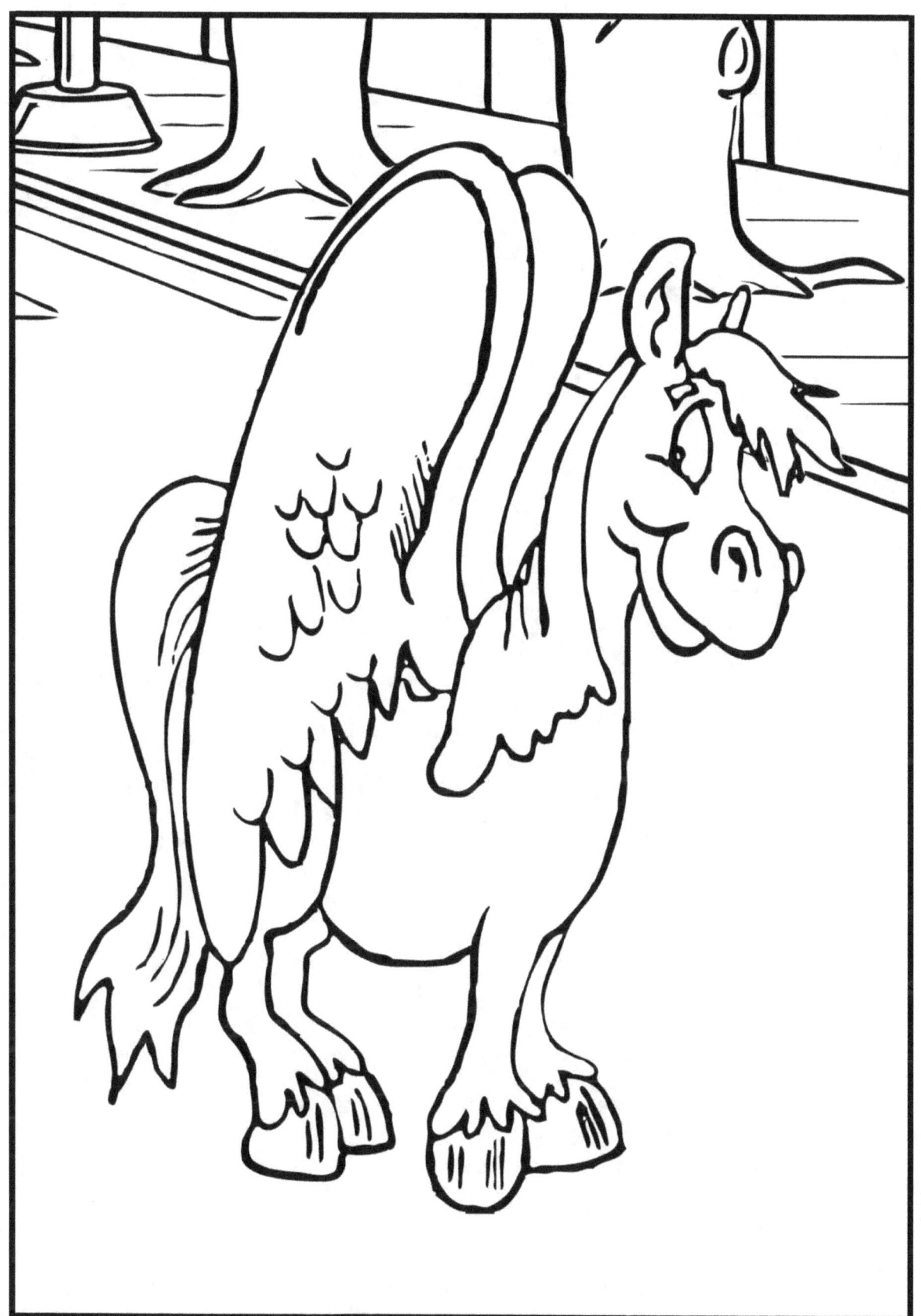

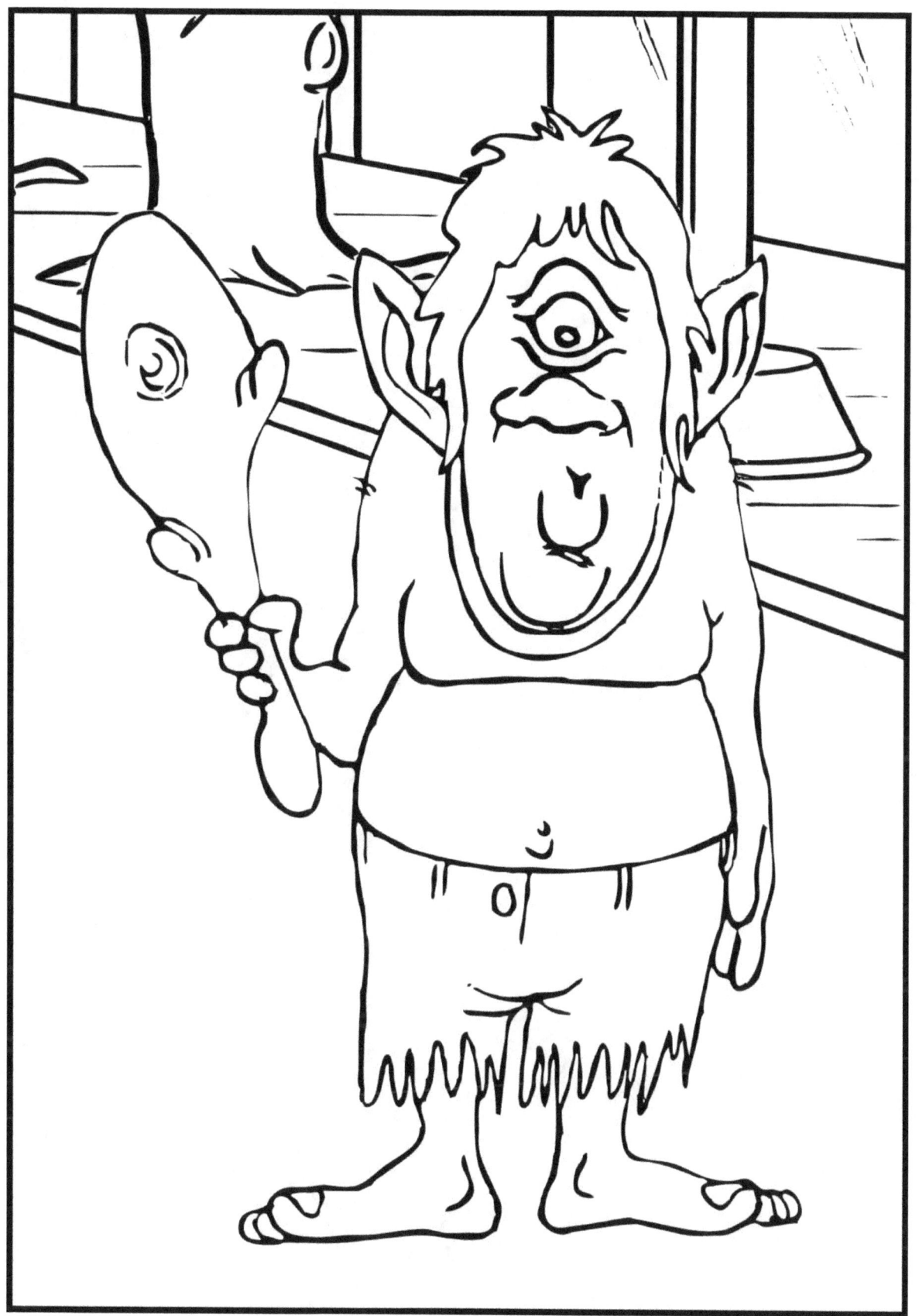

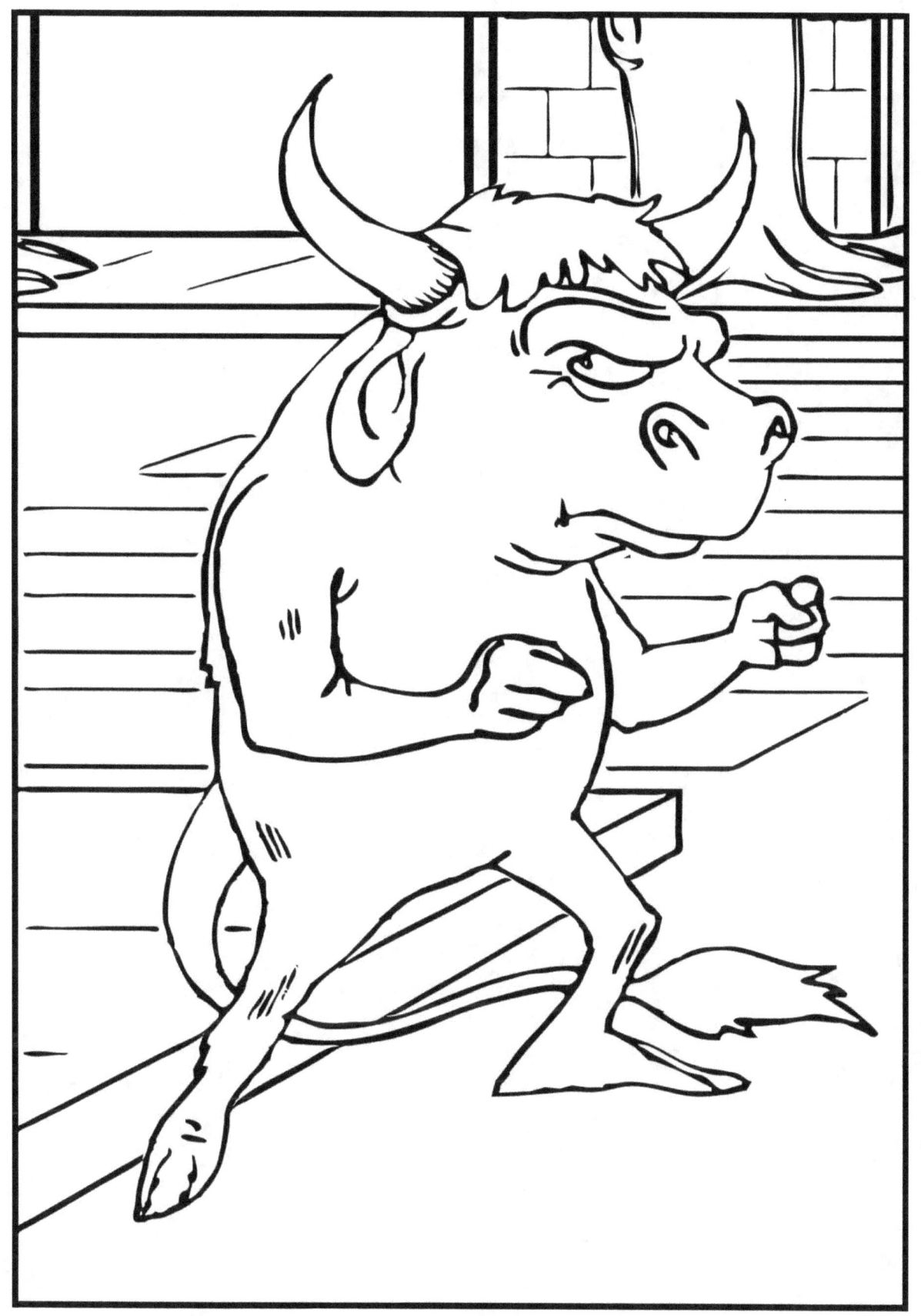

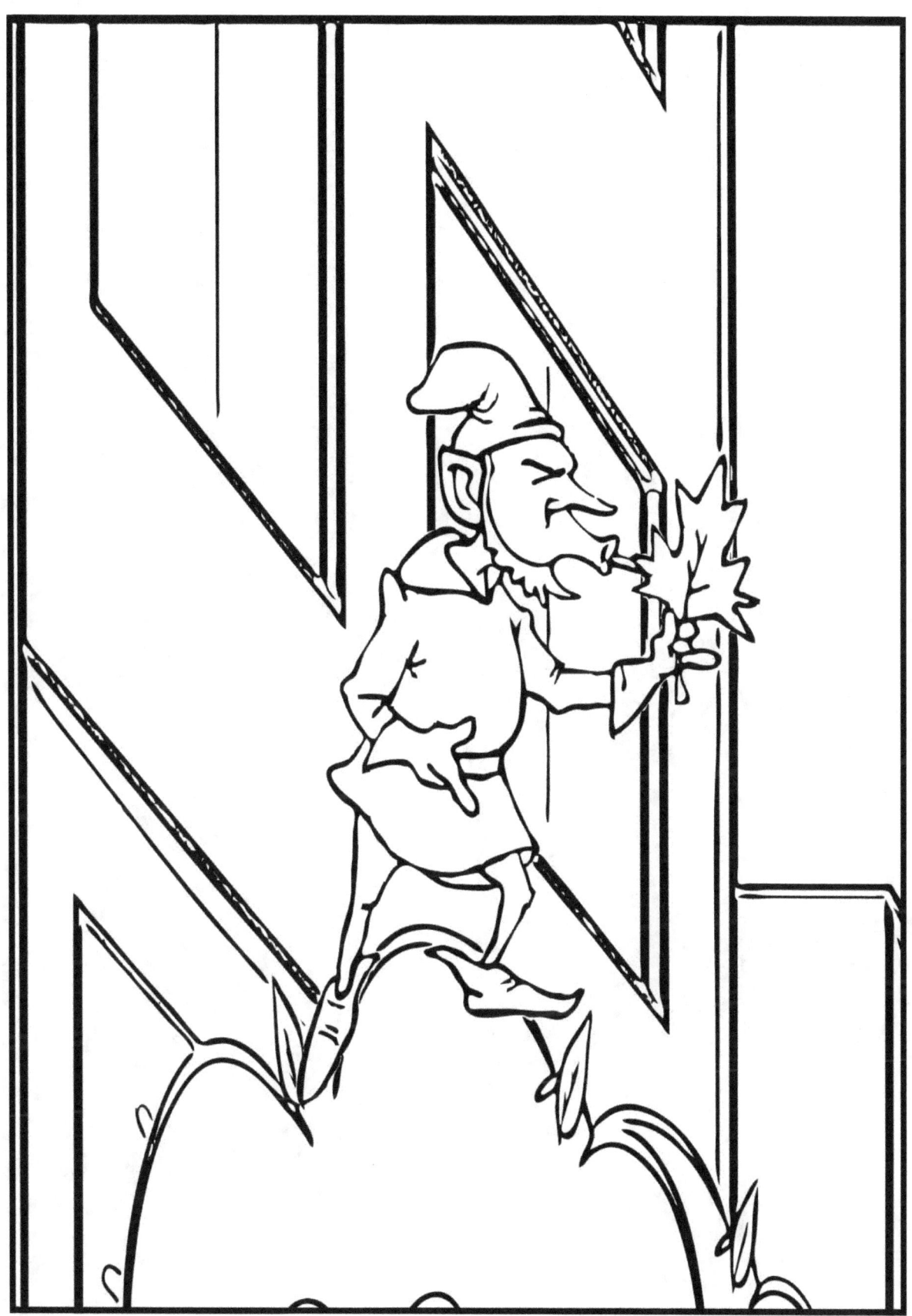

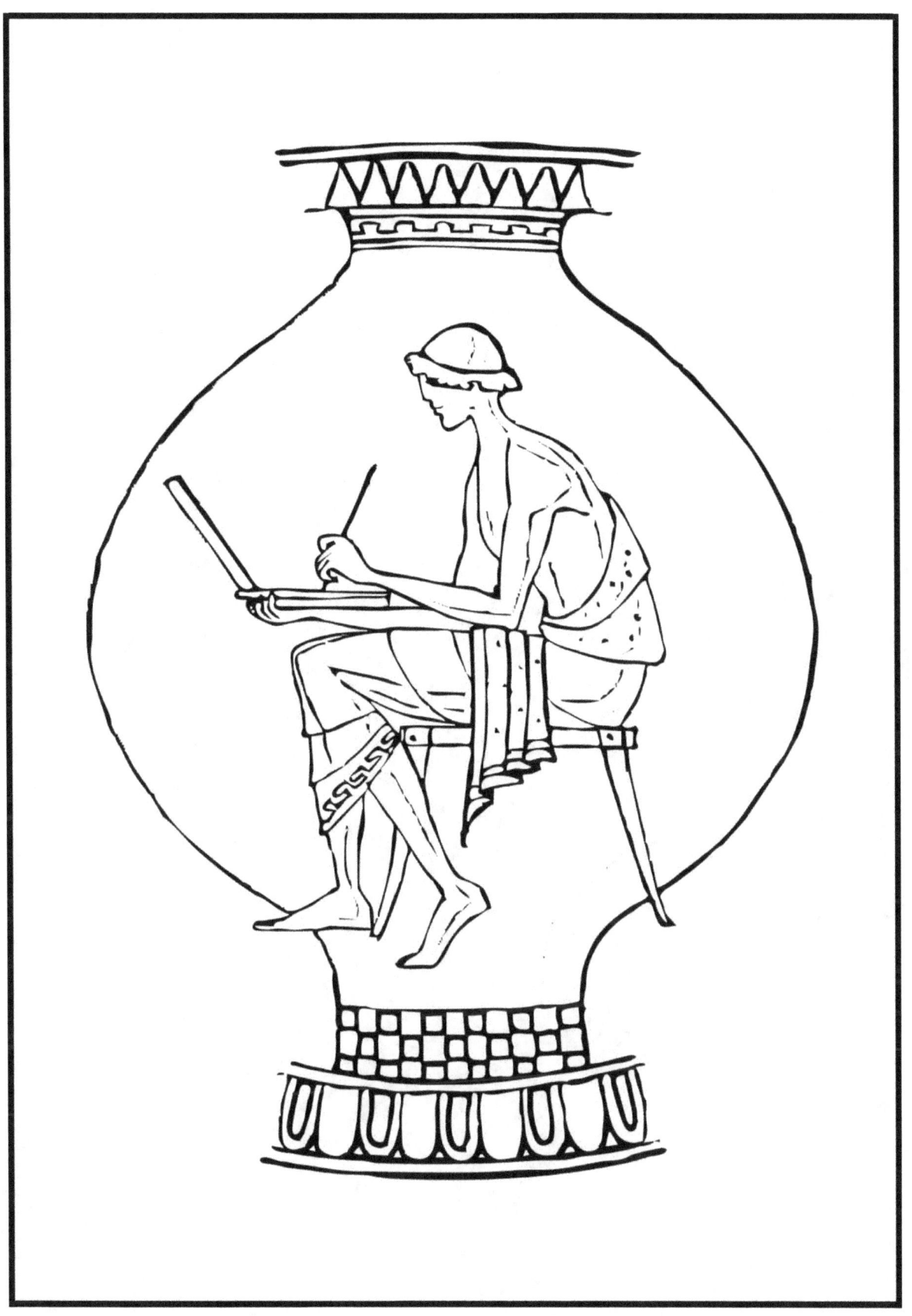

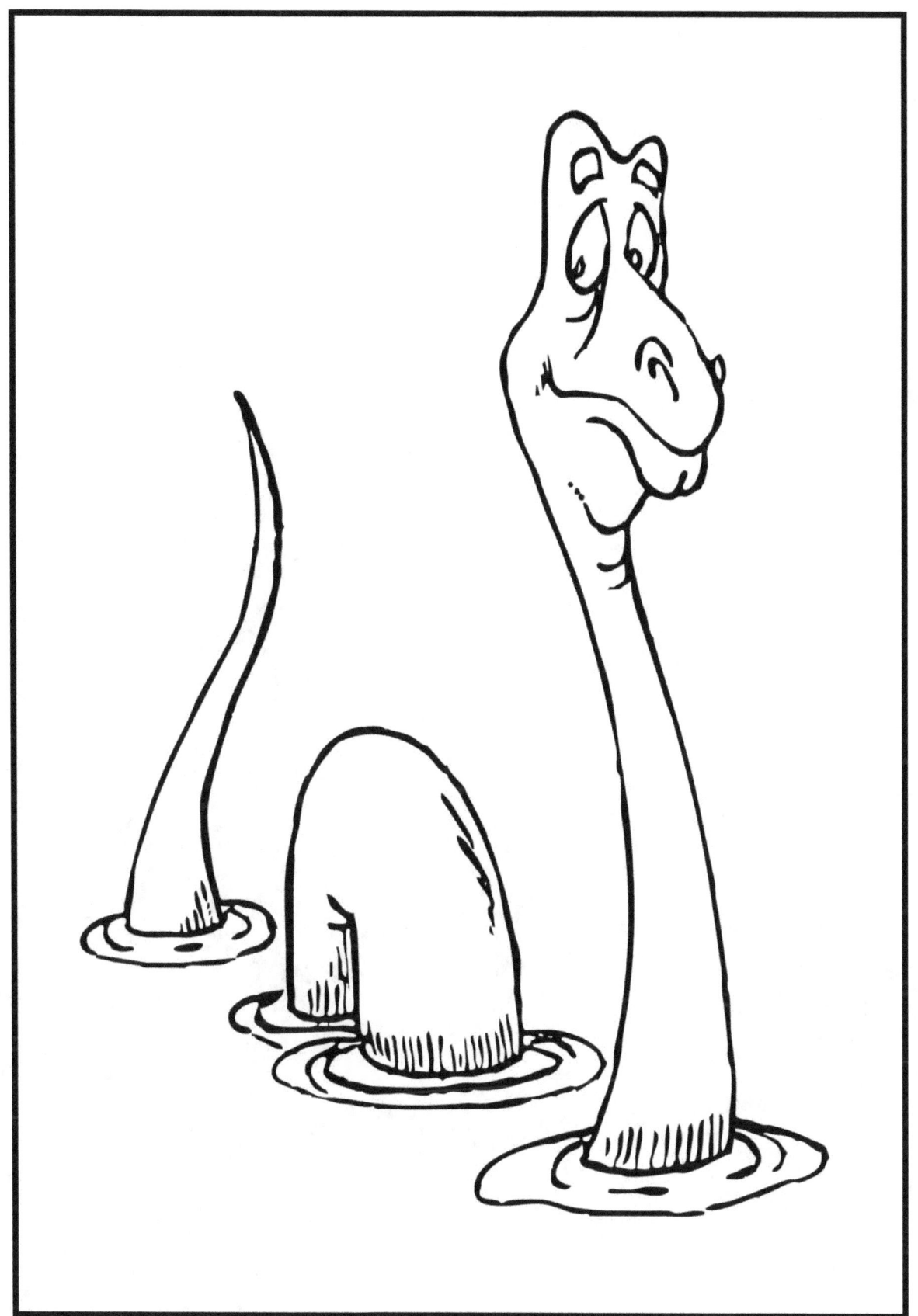

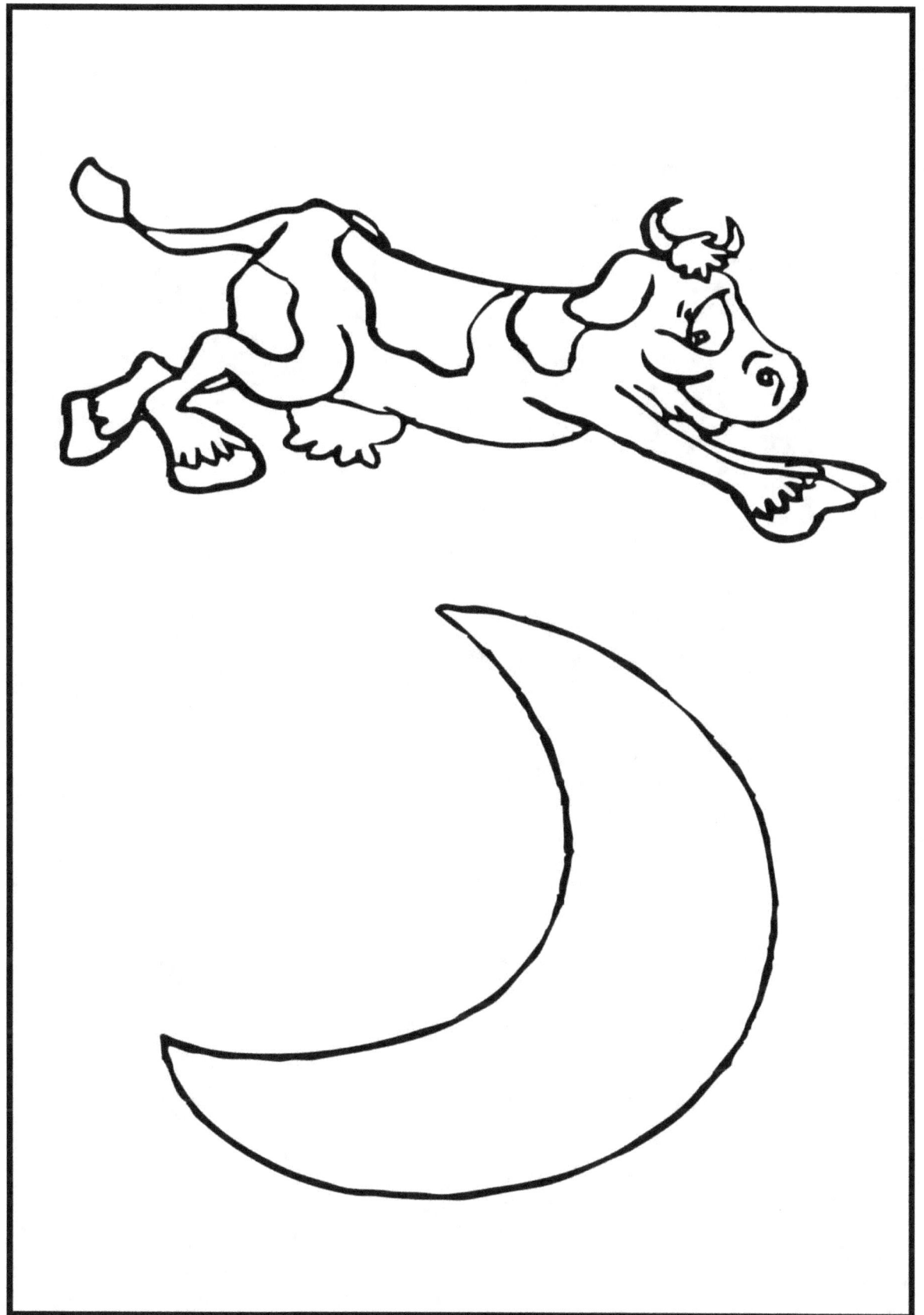

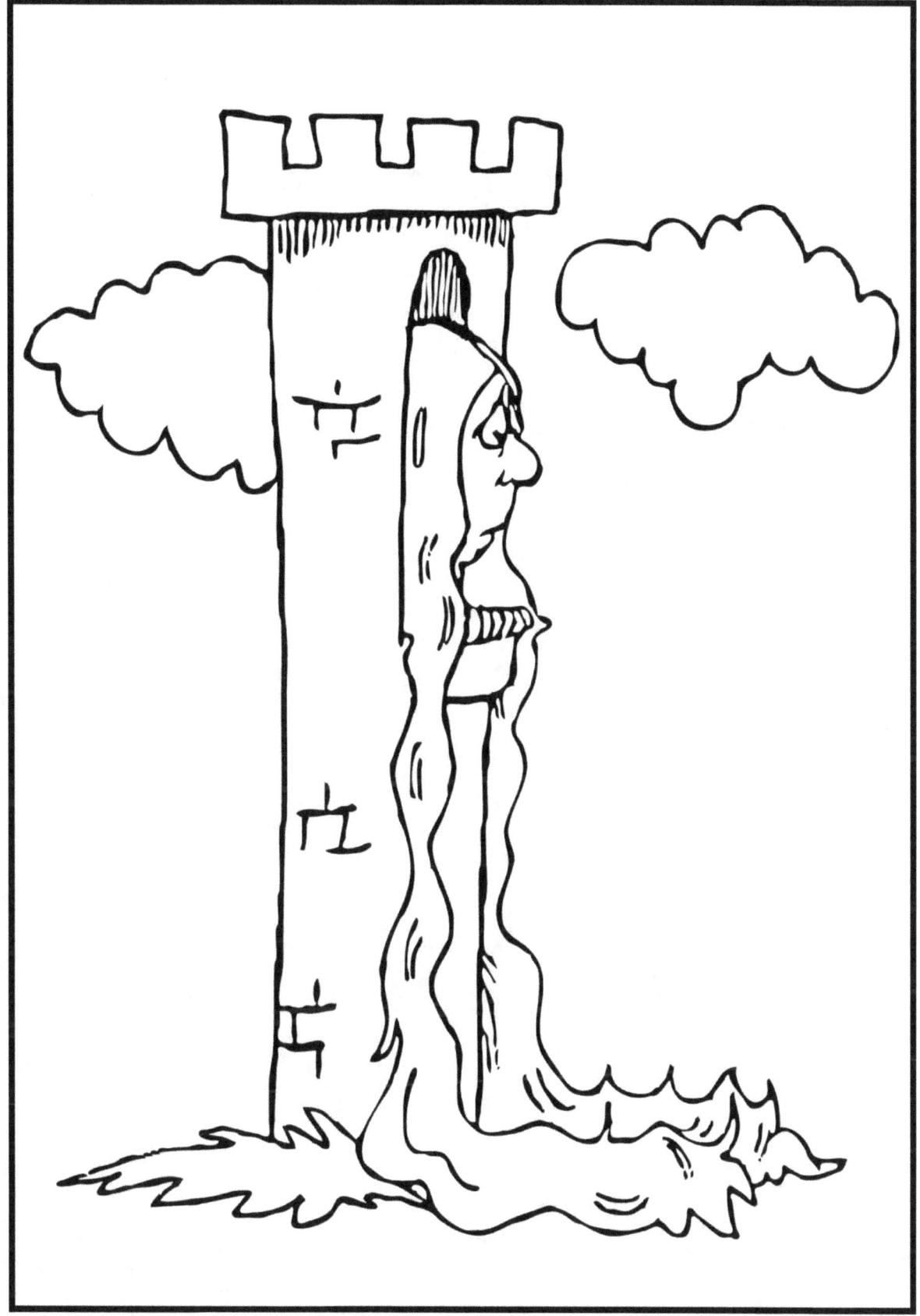

www.ingramcontent.com/pod-product-compliance
Lightning Source LLC
Chambersburg PA
CBHW081557170526
45166CB00009B/2730